PRACTICAL
PAINT EFFECTS
for furniture, fabric and finishing touches

PRACTICAL
PAINT EFFECTS

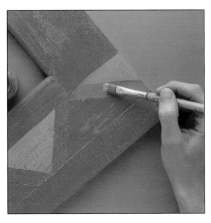

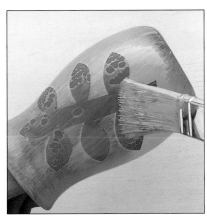

■ Over 25 step-by-step projects for decorating tables, chairs, cabinets, curtains, cushions, napkins, picture frames, vases, candles, flower pots and gift wrap

■ Featuring over 450 colour photographs and expert advice on paint techniques

**Sacha Cohen
and Maggie Philo**

southwater

This edition is published by Southwater

Southwater is an imprint of Anness Publishing Ltd
Hermes House, 88–89 Blackfriars Road, London SE1 8HA
tel. 020 7401 2077; fax 020 7633 9499
www.southwaterbooks.com; info@anness.com

© Anness Publishing Ltd 2006

UK agent: The Manning Partnership Ltd
6 The Old Dairy, Melcombe Road, Bath BA2 3LR
tel. 01225 478444; fax 01225 478440
sales@manning-partnership.co.uk

UK distributor: Grantham Book Services Ltd
Isaac Newton Way, Alma Park Industrial Estate
Grantham, Lincs NG31 9SD
tel. 01476 541080; fax 01476 541061
orders@gbs.tbs-ltd.co.uk

North American agent/distributor: National Book Network
4501 Forbes Boulevard, Suite 200, Lanham, MD 20706
tel. 301 459 3366; fax 301 429 5746
www.nbnbooks.com

Australian agent/distributor: Pan Macmillan Australia
Level 18, St Martins Tower, 31 Market St
Sydney, NSW 2000
tel. 1300 135 113; fax 1300 135 103
customer.service@macmillan.com.au

New Zealand agent/distributor: David Bateman Ltd
30 Tarndale Grove, Off Bush Road, Albany, Auckland
tel. (09) 415 7664; fax (09) 415 8892

A CIP catalogue record for this book is available
from the British Library.

Publisher: Joanna Lorenz
Editorial Director: Judith Simons
Editors: Felicity Forster and Elizabeth Woodland
Copy Editor: Judy Cox
Photographers: Lizzie Orme and Adrian Taylor
Project Contributors: Petra Boase, Sacha Cohen, Lucinda
Ganderton, Elaine Green, Emma Hardy and Liz Wagstaff
Stylists: Katie Gibbs and Judy Williams
Designer: Bill Mason
Cover Designer: Balley Design Associates
Editorial Reader: Jay Thundercliffe
Production Controller: Claire Rae

Previously published as part of a larger volume,
 Complete Paint Effects

10 9 8 7 6 5 4 3 2 1

Bracketed terms are intended for American readers.

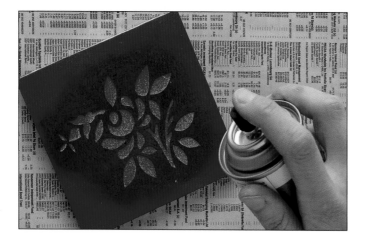

CONTENTS

Introduction   6

**Materials, Equipment and
      Techniques**   8
Painting Materials   10
Stencilling Materials   12
Stamping Materials   14
Painting Equipment   16
Stencilling Equipment   18
Stamping Equipment   20
Painting Techniques   22
Stencilling Techniques   28
Stamping Techniques   33
Stamp Effects   38

The Projects   40
Distressed Table Top   43
Dry-brushed Chair   45
Grained Door   48
Harlequin Screen   50
Scandinavian Table   54
Folk-art Chair   58

Starry Cabinet   61
Grained Window Frame   64
Wax-resist Shutters   66
Vinegar-glazed Floorcloth   69
Crackle-glaze Picture Frame   72
Sponged Lamp Base   76
Crackle-glaze Planter   80
Frosted Vases   82
Art Nouveau Hatbox   85
Star Frame   88
Seashore Bathroom Set   91
Tray of Autumn Leaves   94
Gilded Candles   97
Trompe L'Oeil Plates   100
Spotted Flower Pots   104
Strawberry Fruit Basket   106
Stamped Wrapping Paper   109
French Country Kitchen   112
Organza Cushion   116
Tablecloth and Napkins   119

Templates   122

Index   128

INTRODUCTION

This book brings together the easiest and most adaptable of decorative paint techniques, together with fabulous ideas for applying them to the surfaces of your home. The first part of the book contains a wealth of useful advice on all the basic painting, stencilling and stamping techniques, as well as details of the materials and equipment that you will need to get started. There is clear guidance on mixing your own paint, working with glazes and varnishes, and making your own stencils and stamps. The second part of the book contains twenty-six fun projects, which range from the simple to the more complicated, so there is something for every level of expertise and ability. Each project is explained fully with clear step-by-step instructions and

photographs to guarantee great results. If you are planning to revamp an existing room, you will find ideas for different ways of decorating furniture, picture frames, trays, plant pots, plates, candles and cushions. Why not create an instant grain-effect door, a stunning harlequin screen or an antique-aged scandinavian table? Alternatively, you can use stencils and stamping to make decorative plates, use a simple chequerboard pattern to create French country curtains, or use the sponging technique to make a delightful decorative lamp base. With just a little imagination and a lot of fun, you can add new interest and colour to your home furnishings, and with this compendium of new and innovative decorative projects, you will never be short of inspiration.

MATERIALS, EQUIPMENT AND TECHNIQUES

The following pages show how to create the paint effects that are used in the projects. Detailed information is included on the tools and materials required for each technique, and the methods are described in clear steps to help you produce stunning results. Read through each one before you start, so you know what it entails and the equipment you will need.

PAINTING MATERIALS

Acrylic or emulsion (latex) paint and acrylic scumble glaze are the main painting materials that you will need to put a wide variety of paint techniques into practice.

Acrylic primer is a quick-drying water-based primer. It is used to prime new wood.

Acrylic scumble is a slow-drying, water-based medium with a milky, gel-like appearance, which dries clear. It adds texture and translucency to the paint, and the marks you make with brushes, sponges and other tools are held in the glaze.

Acrylic varnish is available in a satin or matt (flat) finish. It is used to seal paint effects to give a more durable and protective finish to the surface. Acrylic floor varnish is extremely hardwearing and should be used on floors.

Artist's acrylic paint can be found in art and craft shops and comes in a wide range of colours. It gives various paint effects a subtle translucent quality.

Crackle glaze is brushed on to a surface, causing the paint laid over it to crack in random patterns to create an aged appearance.

Emulsion paint is opaque and comes in a choice of matt (flat) or satin finish. Satin finish is best for the base colour and matt for paint effects. Use sample pots of paint if you need only a small amount.

Methylated spirits (methyl alcohol) is a solvent that will dissolve emulsion (latex) paint and can therefore be used to distress paint. It is also used as a solvent, thinner and brush cleaner for shellac.

Pure powder pigment can be used to colour paint and can be mixed with acrylic scumble, clear wax or emulsion (latex) paint. It is also used for vinegar graining.

Shellac is a type of varnish, which is available in clear and brown shades. French polish and button polish are in fact shellac and may be easier to find. Shellac can be used to seal wood, metal leaf and paint.

Wax is available in neutral and in brown. It will seal and colour paint. Neutral wax can be mixed with powder pigment.

RIGHT: 1 powder pigments, 2 emulsion (latex) paints, 3 acrylic primer, 4 artist's acrylic paint, 5 acrylic scumble, 6 crackle glaze, 7 neutral wax, 8 brown wax, 9 methylated spirits (methyl alcohol), 10 brown shellac, 11 clear shellac.

STENCILLING MATERIALS

A variety of materials can be used for stencilling, from specialist stencilling paints and sticks to acrylics and emulsion (latex). Each has its own properties and will create different effects.

Acrylic stencil paints
These are quick-drying paints, reducing the chance of the paint running and seeping behind the stencil. Acrylic stencil paints are available in a wide range of colours and can be mixed to create more subtle shades.

Acrylic varnish
This is useful for sealing and protecting finished projects.

Emulsion paints
Ordinary household emulsion (latex) can also be used for stencilling. It is best to avoid the cheaper varieties as these contain a lot of water and will seep through the stencil.

Fabric paints
These are used in the same way as acrylic stencil paints, and come in an equally wide range of colours, which can be mixed to create your own shades. Fixed with an iron according to the manufacturer's instructions, they will withstand washing and everyday use. As with ordinary acrylic stencil paints do not overload the brush with colour, as it will seep into the fabric. Always back the fabric you are stencilling with scrap paper or newspaper to prevent the paints from marking the work surface.

Gold leaf and gold size
These can be used to spectacular effect. The actual design is stencilled with gold size. The size is then left to become tacky and the gold leaf rubbed over the design.

Metallic creams
These are available in many different metallic finishes, from gold through to bronze and copper and silver. Metallic creams can be applied as highlights on a painted base, or used for the entire design. They can be applied with cloths or your fingertip.

Oil-based stencil sticks and creams
The sticks can be used in the same way as a wax crayon, while the creams can be applied with a brush, cloth or your fingertip. With any method, there is no danger of overloading the colour, and they won't run. The disadvantage is their long drying time (can be overnight in some cases); also, the colours can become muddy when mixed. Sticks and creams are also available for use on fabrics.

RIGHT: 1 acrylic stencil paints, 2 oil-based cream and metallic creams, 3 fabric paints, 4 oil-based stencil sticks, 5 emulsion (latex) paints, 6 gold leaf, 7 acrylic varnish, 8 gold size.

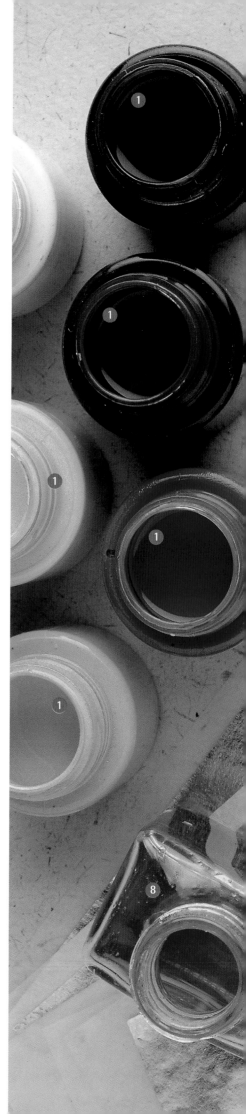

STAMPING MATERIALS

Stamps can be constructed from a variety of materials, and a whole range of exciting and stylish effects can be achieved by combining different paints and inks with your chosen stamps.

Dutch metal leaf and gold size
Metal leaf is a cheap, easy-to-use alternative to real gold leaf. Use a sponge stamp to apply gold size in a repeating pattern. When the size is tacky, apply the gold leaf.

Inks
Water-based inks are too runny to use on their own but can be added to wallpaper paste or varnish to make a mixture thick enough to adhere to the stamp. Use them for paper or card (stock), but not for walls. If you are using rubber stamps, inkpads are commercially available in a range of colours.

Interior filler
Add filler, in its dry powdered state, to emulsion (latex) paint to give it body without diluting the colour.

Paint
Water-based paints such as emulsion and artist's acrylics dry quickly to a permanent finish. Use emulsion paint straight from the can or dilute it with wallpaper paste or varnish. For wall treatments, emulsion paint can be thinned with water and sponged or brushed over the wall as a colourwash.

Pre-cut stamps
Rubber stamps are widely available in thousands of designs. Finely detailed motifs are best suited to small-scale projects, while bolder shapes are best for walls and also furniture.

Sponge or foam
Different types of sponge are characterized by their density. High-density sponge is best for detailed shapes and will give a smooth, sharp print. Medium-density sponge or low-density sponge will absorb more paint and give a more textured result.

Varnish
Use water-based acrylic varnish (sold as quick-drying) for stamping projects. It can be mixed with emulsion paint or ink to thicken the texture and create a range of different sheens. The varnish will also protect and preserve the design of your stamp.

Wallpaper paste
This allows you to thin emulsion paint without making it too runny to adhere to the stamp. Mix up the paste with the required amount of water first, then add the emulsion.

RIGHT: 1 Dutch metal leaf and gold size, 2 coloured inks, 3 low-density sponge, 4 pre-cut stamp, 5 high-density sponge, 6 medium-density sponges, 7 interior filler, 8 emulsion (latex) paint, 9 varnish, 10 wallpaper paste.

PAINTING EQUIPMENT

Different paint effects require different tools. Most of the tools illustrated are cheap and they are easily found in do-it-yourself or decorating suppliers.

Abrasives include abrasive paper and wire (steel) wool, which come in many grades. They are used for distressing paint.

Artist's paintbrushes are needed to paint fine detail.

Decorator's paintbrushes are used to apply emulsion (latex) paint, washes and glazes. They come in a wide range of sizes.

Flat varnish brushes can be used for painting and varnishing. They are often the choice of the experts.

Masking tape comes in many types. Easy-mask and low-tack tapes are less likely to pull off paintwork, and flexible tape is good for going around curves. Fine line tape is useful for creating a narrow negative line.

Measuring equipment such as a ruler, spirit level, set square (T square) and plumbline are needed to mark out designs.

Mutton cloth is very absorbent and can be used for paint effects. Cotton cloths are also used for ragging and polishing.

Natural sponges are used for sponging. They are valued for their textural quality. Synthetic sponges can be used for colourwashing.

Paint containers such as paint kettles, trays and pots are used to mix and store paint.

Paint rollers, small and large, are used to provide an even-textured base colour without brushmarks. They are also used to create textured paint effects.

Rubber combs and heart grainers are used to create textured patterns in paint glazes. Heart grainers (rockers) create an effect of the heart grain of wood.

Softening brushes are used for blending colours together.

Stencil brushes are for stippling paint on to smaller surfaces.

Stippling brushes are usually rectangular, and are used to even out the texture of glaze and to avoid brushmarks.

RIGHT: 1 paint containers, 2 spirit level, 3 plumbline, 4 kitchen paper, 5 artist's brushes, 6 decorator's brushes, 7 flat varnish brushes, 8 hog softening brush, 9 stencil brush, 10 paint rollers, 11 gloves, 12 stippling brush, 13 masking tapes, 14 measuring equipment, 15 craft knife and pencil, 16 heart grainer (rocker), 17 combs, 18 natural and synthetic sponges, 19 mutton cloth (stockinet), 20 rag, 21 wire (steel) wool and abrasive paper.

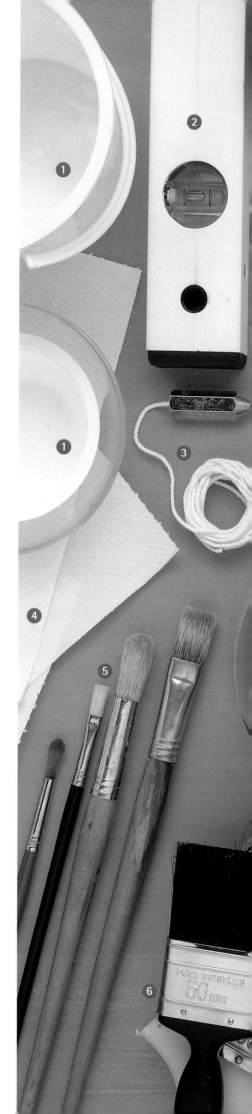

STENCILLING EQUIPMENT

Stencilling does not require a great deal of specialist equipment; many of the items used are commonly found in most households. Some additional items, however, will make the job easier.

Brushes

It is worth investing in a set of good stencil brushes. The ends of the brushes should be flat and the bristles firm, to allow you to control the application of paint. A medium-sized brush (3cm/1½in diameter) is a useful, all-purpose size, but you may want to buy one size smaller and one size larger as well. You will need a selection of household paintbrushes for applying large areas of background colour, and small artist's paintbrushes for adding fine details.

Craft knife

Use for cutting out stencils from card (stock).

Self-healing cutting mat

This provides a firm surface to cut into and will help prevent the craft knife from slipping. Mats come in a range of sizes and are commonly printed with a grid and imperial or metric measures for accurate and quick cutting.

Masking tape

As the stencil may need to be repositioned it is advisable to hold it in place with masking tape, which can be removed fairly easily.

Paint-mixing container

This may be necessary for mixing paints and colourwashes.

Pencils

Keep a selection of both soft and hard pencils to transfer the stencil design on to card (stock). Use an ordinary pencil to mark the positions of the stencils before applying.

Stencil card

The material used to make the stencil is a matter of personal preference. Special stencil card (stock) is available waxed, which means that it will last longer, but ordinary card or heavy paper can also be used. It is worth purchasing a sheet of clear acetate if you wish to keep your stencil design. This means that you will be able to reuse the design for future projects.

Tape measure and straight-edges

Many stencilling projects require accurate positioning. Measuring and planning the design and layout of your stencils before you begin will aid the result.

Tracing paper

Use this to transfer your stencil design on to stencil card (stock).

RIGHT: 1 sraight-edges, 2 tape measure, 3 stencil brushes, 4 household paintbrush, 5 self-healing cutting mat, 6 stencil card (stock), 7 tracing paper, 8 soft pencil, 9 craft knife, 10 paint-mixing container, 11 masking tape.

STAMPING EQUIPMENT

Stamping is a very simple craft and does not require a great deal of specialist equipment. Most of the items illustrated here will already be found in an ordinary household.

Craft knife and self-healing cutting mat
A sharp-bladed craft knife is essential for cutting your own stamps out of sponge. Use a self-healing cutting mat to protect your work surface, and always direct the blade away from your fingers.

Linoleum blocks
These are available from art and craft shops and can be cut to make stamps which recreate the look of a wood block. You'll need special linoleum-cutting tools, which are also easily available, to scoop out the areas around the design. Always hold the linoleum with your spare hand behind your cutting hand for safety.

Masking tape
Use for masking off areas of walls and furniture.

Natural sponge
Use for applying colourwashes to walls and other larger surfaces before stamping.

Paintbrushes
A range of decorator's brushes is needed for painting furniture and walls before stamping. Use a broad brush to apply colourwashes to walls. Stiff brushes can be used to stipple paint on to stamps for textured effects, while finer brushes are used to pick out details or to apply paint to the stamp.

Pencils, pens and crayons
Use a soft pencil to trace templates for stamps, and for making easily removable guidelines on walls. Draw motifs freehand using a felt-tipped pen on medium- and low-density sponge. Use a white crayon on black upholstery foam.

Rags
Keep a stock of clean rags and cloths for cleaning stamps and preparing surfaces.

Ruler and tape measure
Use these to plan your design.

Scissors
Use sharp scissors to cut out medium- and low-density sponge shapes and also for cutting out templates.

Sponge rollers
Small paint rollers can be used to load your stamps. You will need several if you are stamping in different colours.

RIGHT: 1 scissors, 2 craft knife, 3 masking tape, 4 paint rollers, 5 ruler, 6 tape measure, 7 pencils, 8 self-healing cutting mat, 9 rag, 10 natural sponge, 11 paintbrushes.

PAINTING TECHNIQUES

Most of the projects in this chapter are based on a few simple techniques. These can be used on their own, or combined to produce an infinite variety of paint effects. The techniques shown here all use ultramarine blue emulsion (latex) paint. This has been mixed with acrylic scumble glaze and/or water, as appropriate, to achieve the desired effect. Two coats of satin finish white emulsion paint were rollered on as a base. This provides an even-textured, non-absorbent finish, which is ideal to work on as it allows glazes to dry more slowly and evenly than emulsion paint. It also means that if you make any mistakes they are easily wiped off. All these techniques, except the crackle glaze, can be done with artist's acrylic paint mixed with scumble, in which case the effects will look more translucent.

Sponging

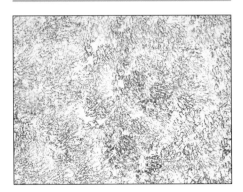

Dilute a little paint with a little water in a paint tray or on a saucer. Dip a damp natural sponge into the paint and wipe off the excess on kitchen paper. Dab the sponge evenly on to the prepared surface in different directions.

Sponging and dispersion

Follow the technique as for sponging, then rinse the sponge in clean water and dab it over the sponged paint before it dries to soften the effect.

Combing

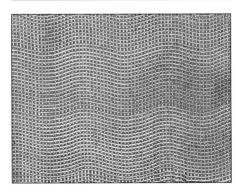

Mix the paint with acrylic scumble and brush on with cross-hatched brushstrokes. Run a metal or rubber graining comb through the wet glaze to make a pattern. This pattern was done with straight vertical strokes followed by wavy horizontal ones.

Colourwashing

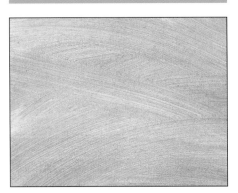

Dilute the paint with water and brush on randomly with cross-hatched brushstrokes, using a large decorator's brush. Alternatively, a damp sponge will give a similar effect.

Rubbing in colourwash

Dilute the paint with water and brush on. Use a clean cotton rag to disperse the paint. Alternatively, apply it directly with the rag and rub in.

Frottage

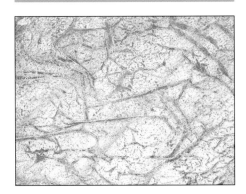

Apply paint with cross-hatched brushstrokes, then press a piece of tissue paper over the wet surface and peel it off. The paint can be diluted with water or scumble.

Dabbing with a mutton cloth

Brush on paint mixed with scumble, using cross-hatched brushstrokes. Dab a mutton cloth (stockinet) over the wet glaze to even out the texture and eliminate the brushstrokes.

Ragging

Mix paint with scumble and brush on, using cross-hatched brushstrokes. Scrunch up a piece of cotton rag and dab this on the wet paint in all directions, twisting your hand for a random look. When the rag becomes too paint-soaked, use a new one.

Rag rolling without brushmarks

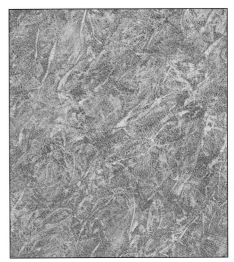

Brush on paint mixed with scumble and dab with a mutton cloth (stockinet) to eliminate brushmarks. Scrunch a cotton rag into a sausage shape and roll over the surface, changing direction as you go. Use a new piece of rag when it becomes too wet.

Stippling

Brush on paint mixed with acrylic scumble, using cross-hatched brushstrokes. Pounce a stippling brush over the wet glaze, working from the bottom upwards to eliminate brushmarks and provide an even-textured surface. Keep the brush as dry as possible by regularly wiping the bristles with kitchen paper.

Dragging

Mix paint with scumble glaze and brush on with cross-hatched brushstrokes. Drag a flat decorator's brush through the wet glaze, keeping a steady hand. The soft effect shown here is achieved by going over the wet glaze a second time to break up the vertical lines.

Crackle glaze

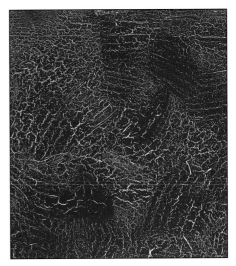

Brush on a coat of water-based crackle glaze and leave to dry according to the manufacturer's instructions. Using a well-laden brush, apply paint carefully on top so that you lay, rather than brush, it over the surface. Work quickly and do not overbrush an area already painted. If you have missed an area, touch it in when the paint has dried. Seal with acrylic varnish.

MIXING PAINTS AND GLAZES

There are no precise recipes for mixing glazes and washes. Generally, the proportion of emulsion (latex) paint to scumble is 1 part paint to 6 parts scumble. This will give soft, semi-translucent colour that is suitable for effects such as ragging, dragging and combing where you want the coloured glaze to hold the marks you have made. You can reduce the amount of scumble if you want a more opaque coverage. However the paint will dry more quickly so it may be harder to maintain a wet edge for an even result. When you are mixing scumble with artist's acrylic paint, the amount of paint you should use depends on the depth of colour you need. Acrylic paint mixed with scumble gives a more translucent colour. It is used in exactly the same way as the emulsion glazes and washes.

If you do not need the texture provided by the scumble (for example, when colourwashing) but you want to dilute the colour, use water. This is cheaper but it dries more quickly, which may be a disadvantage. If you want to slow down the drying time, add a 50/50 mix of water and scumble to the paint. Emulsion paint can be diluted with any amount of water, and several thin washes of colour will give a more even cover than one thick wash.

Try to mix up enough colour to complete the area you are to decorate. Washes and glazes stretch a long way, but if in doubt, mix up more than you think you might need. If you want to repeat the effect, measure the quantities you use. Before you start, painting samples on to scrap wood will give you the truest effect.

Ragging with acrylic paint and scumble.

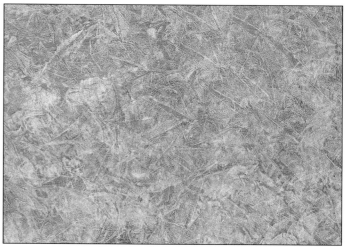

Ragging with emulsion (latex) paint and scumble.

Colourwashing with one wash of equal parts emulsion (latex) paint and water.

Colourwashing with four thin washes of 1 part paint to 8 parts water to achieve the same colour saturation.

WORKING WITH COLOUR

Paint effects can vary widely according to your choice of colour and the way in which you use it. Whether you put a light colour over a dark base or a dark colour over a light one is a matter of choice, although a translucent pale colour would not really be visible over a dark base. A bright base colour can give added depth and a subtle glow beneath a dark top coat, while using the colours the other way round will tone down a bright colour. Tone-on-tone colour combinations are good for a subtle effect and are always a safe bet, but experiment with contrasting colours for exciting results.

Many of the techniques in this section use layers of several different colours. Greater depth and texture are achieved when you build up colours in this way, but a simple technique with one colour can be just as effective. It depends on the look you want and the furnishings in the room.

If you want to tone down a paint effect, you can lighten it by brushing over a wash of very diluted white or off-white emulsion (latex) paint. You can also tone down a colour by darkening it. A wash of raw umber paint works well over most colours and has a much warmer feel than black.

Adding white to lighten bright blue colourwashing.

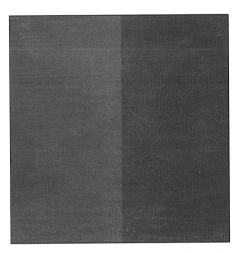

Adding raw umber to darken bright red colourwashing.

Sponging – light yellow over deep yellow (left), deep yellow over light yellow (right).

Dabbing with a mutton cloth (stockinet) – dull green over emerald green (left), emerald green over dull green (right).

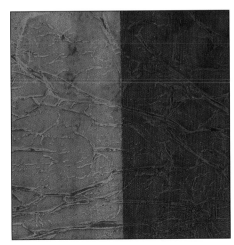

Frottage – tone-on-tone, deep blue over light blue (left), two tones of contrasting colours, bright blue over orange (right).

Colourwashing (left) in orange, red and crimson, finishing with the darkest colour on the top surface. Layers of sponging (right) in three shades of blue-green, finishing with the lightest colour on the top surface.

MIXING COLOURS

Emulsion (latex) paint is available in a huge range of ready-mixed colours. If you use acrylic paint or pure powder pigment you will need to mix your own colours.

Most colours can be mixed from yellow, cyan blue, magenta, black and white, but a basic palette of 14 colours plus black and white will allow you to mix an enormous range of colours. The suggested palette consists of yellow ochre, cadmium yellow, raw sienna, burnt sienna, red ochre, cadmium red, alizarin crimson, ultramarine blue, Prussian blue, cerulean blue, viridian green, oxide of chromium, raw umber and burnt umber. These basic colours are beautiful alone, and many other colours can be made by mixing them.

Some colour combinations are unexpected, and there are no hard-and-fast rules about which colours should or should not be mixed. If you experiment, you will soon develop confidence and a good eye for mixing colour.

Yellows and browns (right)

1 Cadmium yellow and white

2 Cadmium yellow

3 Cadmium yellow and
*   viridian green*

4 Yellow ochre and white

5 Yellow ochre

6 Raw sienna

7 Burnt sienna

8 Burnt umber

9 Raw umber

Reds

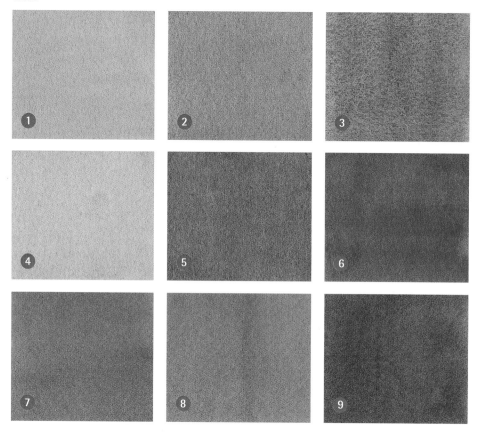

Yellows and browns

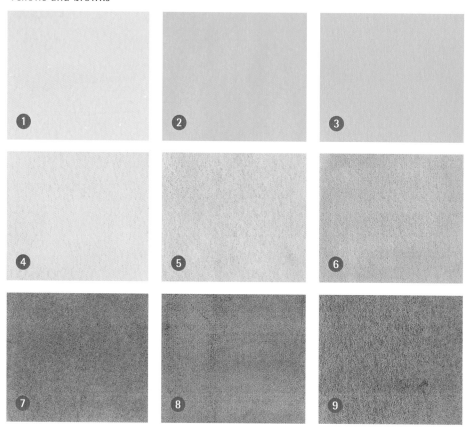

Reds (opposite)

1 *Alizarin crimson, cadmium yellow and white*
2 *Cadmium red and cadmium yellow*
3 *Red ochre*
4 *Red ochre and white*
5 *Cadmium red and burnt umber*
6 *Cadmium red*
7 *Cadmium red and black*
8 *Alizarin crimson*
9 *Alizarin crimson and oxide of chromium*

Blues (top right)

1 *Cerulean blue, raw umber and white*
2 *Prussian blue, black and white*
3 *Prussian blue*
4 *Cerulean blue*
5 *Ultramarine blue and white*
6 *Ultramarine blue*
7 *Alizarin crimson, ultramarine blue and white*
8 *Alizarin crimson and ultramarine blue*
9 *Ultramarine blue and raw umber*

Greens (right)

1 *Prussian blue and yellow ochre*
2 *Prussian blue and cadmium yellow*
3 *Prussian blue, cadmium yellow and white*
4 *Ultramarine and yellow ochre*
5 *Oxide of chromium*
6 *Viridian green and cadmium yellow*
7 *Viridian green*
8 *Viridian green, raw umber and white*
9 *Prussian blue, yellow ochre and white*

Blues

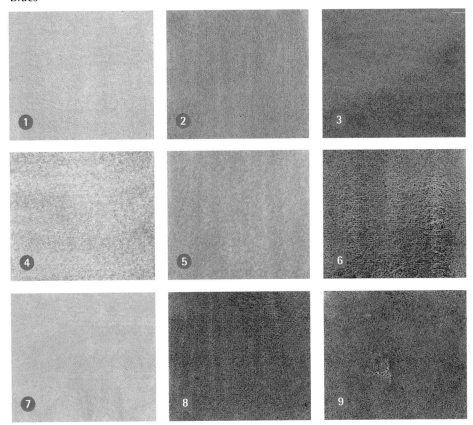

Greens

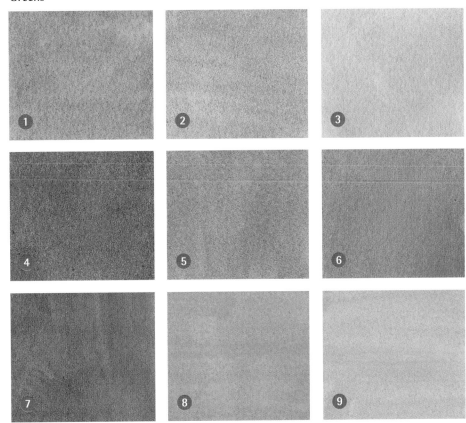

STENCILLING TECHNIQUES

Stencilling is not difficult to master, but it is worth practising on a small area to get used to handling the stencil brush and to become accustomed to the properties of the various paints you use. The techniques illustrated below show you how to make your own stencils and different ways in which to use them.

TRANSFERRING TEMPLATES

1 To transfer a template on to a piece of stencil card (stock), place a piece of tracing paper over the design, and draw over it with a hard pencil.

2 Turn over the tracing paper, and on the back of the design rub over the lines you have drawn, this time using a soft pencil.

3 Turn the design back to the right side and place on a sheet of stencil card. Draw over the original lines with a hard pencil.

CUTTING STENCILS

1 Place the tracing paper design on to a self-healing cutting mat or piece of thick card (stock) and secure in place with masking tape. Use a craft knife for cutting along the pencil lines.

2 It is safer to move the cutting board towards you and the craft knife when you are working round awkward shapes. Continue to cut out the design, moving the board as necessary.

STENCILLING EFFECTS

Block stencilling in a single solid colour

Use for filling in large areas in a single solid colour. As in all stencilling, remember not to apply the paint too heavily – less is more. Always blot out the paint on to a piece of blotting card (stock) before you begin.

Block stencilling with second colour stippled

When applying two colours, always apply the lighter shade first, then the darker. Do not cover the entire surface with the first colour; leave a gap for the second shade, then blend later. Use a separate, clean brush for each colour.

Block stencilling in two colours

When you apply the first colour, do not fully block out the petals; instead, outline them with the first colour and leave the centres bare. Use the second colour to fill. Take care not to apply the paint too heavily.

Rotating with blocked leaves

Using a very dry brush with a tiny amount of paint, rotate the bristles in a circular motion. This rotating action leaves enough paint on the surface for a lighter, softer look than a block application. Use the same effect in a darker colour on the inside of the petals.

Rotating and soft shading

Using a very dry brush with a tiny amount of paint, place your brush on one side of the stencil and rotate the brush in small circles. Repeat this action, using a slightly darker colour on the edges of the stencil, to create the effect of soft shading.

Rotating and shading in two colours

This is a similar effect to rotating and shading, but is more directional. Using a very dry brush with a tiny amount of paint, place your brush in the centre of the flower and rotate the bristles slightly outwards. Repeat this action, using a slightly darker colour.

Brushing up and down

Using slightly more paint on your brush than you would for rotating, brush up and down only, taking care to keep the lines vertical.

Dry brushing with curve

Using the rotating technique, start at the centre of the design and work outwards in big circles.

Dry brushing and rotating

Apply a tiny amount of paint by rotating the bristles from the centre, and from the outside tips, to give more paint in these areas. Work along the line, using less pressure than on the centre and the tips. This gives a softer effect on the areas in between.

Rotating brush with leaves flicked

Fill in the petals by rotating a very dry brush and a tiny amount of paint. For the flicking effect on the leaves, use slightly more paint on the brush. Working from the centre, flick the paint outwards once or twice. Do not overdo.

Dry brushing, rotating from edge

Using big circular strokes, work from the outside of the whole stencil, moving inwards. This should leave you with more paint on the outside, as there will be less and less paint on your brush as you move inwards.

Brushing up and down from the sides

This is similar to flicking. Using slightly more paint on your brush than you would for rotating, brush up and down, then from side to side. Keep the brushmarks vertical and horizontal to give a lined effect.

Rough stippling

This method uses more paint and less pressure than rotating or flicking. Taking a reasonable amount of paint on the bristles of your brush, simply place it down lightly. This gives a rougher look. Do not go over it too many times as this spoils the effect.

Two-colour stippling

Use less paint than for rough stippling. The second colour is stippled out from the centre, to blend with the first colour.

One-sided stippling

Apply the lighter colour first, up to a point just past the centre. Apply the darker colour, and stipple to the centre. Always start on the outer edge so that you leave more paint on the edges of the stencil design.

Stippling with a dry brush

This is similar to stippling, except that it is essential to dab most of the paint off the bristles before you start. This gives a softer stippling effect.

Gentle stippling from the edges

Using a very dry brush (dab most of the paint off the bristles before you start), stipple from the outside, working inwards. By the time you get to the centre, there should be hardly any paint left on your brush, ensuring a very soft paint effect in this area.

Stippling to shade with two colours

Using a reasonable amount of paint, apply the lighter shade first. Apply the darker shade to one side only of each window. (Here, the second colour is applied to the right-hand side.) A few dabs of the darker colour paint will be quite sufficient.

Flicking upwards with the brush

Using a reasonable amount of paint (not too wet or too dry) on your brush, flick upwards only. This creates a line at the top of the petals and leaves.

Flicking in two directions, up and down

Using a reasonable amount of paint on your brush, flick up and down. Do not use too much paint as it will collect on the edges of the petals and leaves.

Flicking from the outside to the centre

Using a reasonable amount of paint on your brush, flick from the outside edges in to the centre of the design. Flick from the top to the centre, from the bottom to the centre, from the left to the centre, and from the right to the centre.

Flicking from the top to the centre

Using a reasonable amount of paint on your brush, flick from the top edge of the window to the centre of the design, then from the bottom edge of the window to the centre.

Drop shadow, using a block effect

Apply the first colour, which should be the lighter shade, using a block effect. Concentrate on one side of each window (here, the right-hand side). Move the stencil slightly to the left – a few millimetres is sufficient – taking care not to move it up or down. Block again, using a darker colour, to create a drop shadow effect.

TIPS

Check the amount of paint on the stencil brush by practising on a piece of scrap paper. Excess paint can be removed by dabbing the brush on an old saucer or clean cotton cloth.

Clean the stencil brush before using a different colour to keep the colours fresh. It is a good idea to invest in several different-sized brushes.

If you want to use a different colour scheme to that shown in the project, for example to suit your existing decor, see Working with Colour at the beginning of the book for advice and inspiration.

Finally, do not aim for perfectly identical stencilled motifs. Much of the appeal of stencilling lies in its handpainted look and irregularities.

STAMPING TECHNIQUES

Stamping is a quick and effective method of repeating a design on a wide variety of surfaces, using many different mixtures of paints and inks. Ready-made stamps are widely available, usually mounted on wooden blocks, but they are also easy to make yourself using foam or sponge.

MAKING STAMPS

1 Use high-density sponge to create sharply defined and detailed designs. Trace your chosen motif using a soft pencil to give dark, clear lines.

2 Roughly cut around the design, then spray the piece of tracing paper with adhesive to hold it in place on the sponge while you are cutting it out.

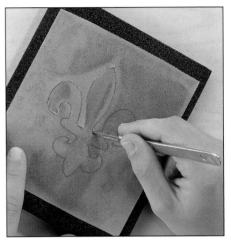

3 Cut along the outline of the motif using a craft knife, then, pinching the background sections, cut them away holding the blade away from your fingers.

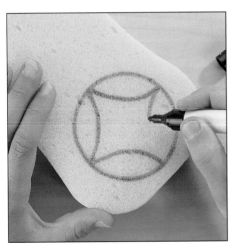

4 The surface of low-density sponge is too soft to use tracing paper as a guide for cutting out the stamp. It is easier to draw the design straight on to the sponge using a felt-tipped pen.

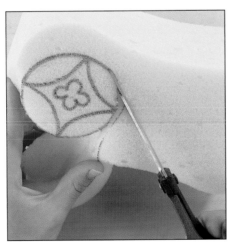

5 Sharp scissors can be used to cut out stamps made from low-density sponge and they are especially useful for cutting out the basic shapes of the motif.

6 As with high-density sponge, the unwanted background areas should be cut away with a craft knife when the outline has been cut, but care is needed as this sponge will tear more easily. Rinse the completed stamp to remove the remains of the felt-tipped pen ink.

PAINT MIXTURES

Wallpaper paste and emulsion paint

Add 50 per cent paste to the emulsion (latex) paint to give a watercolour effect without producing a mixture that is too runny to work with. Apply the mixture using a roller, sponge or paintbrush, or dip the stamp into the paint on a flat plate.

Wallpaper paste and ink

Wallpaper paste thickens the texture of ink, while keeping the rich colour. The effect produced depends on the proportion of ink in the mixture. It will give a more even spread of colour than using emulsion (latex). Apply using a roller or paintbrush.

Varnish and emulsion paint

The density of the emulsion (latex) paint is diluted as with wallpaper paste, but this can also be used to create different sheens according to the type of varnish used. Apply with a roller, paintbrush or sponge, or dip the stamp into the paint on a plate.

Varnish and ink

This effect is similar to the wallpaper paste mixture, but creates a smoother mix as both materials are fine in texture. Again, different sheens can be obtained depending on the varnish used. Apply with a roller.

Wallpaper paste and woodstain

The wallpaper paste dilutes the colour density of the woodstain while thickening the mixture for ease of use. Use quick-drying, water-based woodstains, which are available in a range of colours. Apply with a roller.

Interior filler and emulsion paint

This mixture thickens the paint as opposed to diluting the colour, and is good for creating relief effects. Apply the mixture generously, using a paintbrush, or dip the stamp into the paint on a plate.

HOW TO APPLY PAINT

Using a roller

Pour a little paint on to the side of a flat plate, then, using a small sponge roller, pick up a small amount of paint and roll it out over the rest of the plate until you have an even covering. Roll the paint on to the stamp.

Using a paintbrush

Use a fairly stiff brush and apply the paint with a dabbing or stippling motion. This technique enables more than one colour to be applied and for detail to be picked out. Be careful not to overload the stamp, as this may cause it to slip when stamping.

Dipping into paint on a plate

Brush a thin coat of paint on to a flat plate, then press the stamp into the paint. You may need to do this several times to get an even coating. Initially the stamp will absorb a good amount of paint. Keep brushing more paint on to the plate as you work.

Using a roller and brush

Use a sponge roller to apply the paint evenly over the whole stamp. Use a brush to apply a second colour to act as a highlight or shadow, or to pick out details of the design.

Using a sponge

Spread an even coating of paint on a plate, then use a natural sponge to pick up the paint and dab it on to the stamp. This method allows you to put a light, even covering of paint on to the stamp.

Using an inkpad

Press the stamp lightly on to the inkpad. You may need to do this several times to ensure a good covering. It is difficult to overload the stamp using inkpads. This technique will give a dry look to the stamped motifs.

PREPARING SURFACES

Tiles, china and glass

These are all prepared in the same way, using soapy water to remove dirt and grease, then drying with a lint-free cloth. Appropriate special paints, such as enamel or ceramic paints, must be used as normal emulsion (latex) and acrylic paints will not adhere well and are not sufficiently durable for these surfaces. It is often necessary to strengthen the finished design by applying a coat of varnish.

1 Wash the tile or glass with soapy water and rinse thoroughly. To remove any remaining traces of grease, give the surface a final wipe with a cloth dipped in methylated spirits (methyl alcohol) and leave to dry.

2 When printing on a curved surface, carefully roll the stamp while holding the object securely. Sponge stamps are best suited for this purpose. Rubber stamps are less suitable.

Fabrics

Fabrics must be washed and ironed before stamping to remove any dressing and allow for any shrinkage. Use special fabric paint or ink so that the item can be washed after stamping. Fix the paint to the fabric according to the manufacturer's instructions.

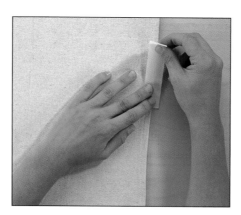

1 Once ironed, lay the fabric on a flat surface and tape down the edges to hold it firmly in position.

2 Place a piece of card (stock) or scrap paper under the area to be stamped to stop any of the paint bleeding through the fabric.

Wood

Wood should be lightly sanded before stamping and varnished afterwards. New wood should be sealed with a coat of shellac to stop resin leaking through the grain. When using woodstains, keep the stamp quite dry to stop the stain bleeding into the grain of the wood.

1 Sand the surface of the wood, then wipe down with a soft cloth to remove any loose dust.

2 Once dry, the stamped design can be rubbed back with abrasive paper to create a distressed effect.

PLANNING A DESIGN

1 With the aid of a spirit level, draw a faint pencil line to use as a guide when stamping.

2 Stamp the motif several times on scrap paper and cut out the prints. Tape them to the wall so that you can judge how your design will look.

3 When using a stamp mounted on a block, you can draw a straight line on the back to help with positioning. Align the block with the pencil guideline on the wall.

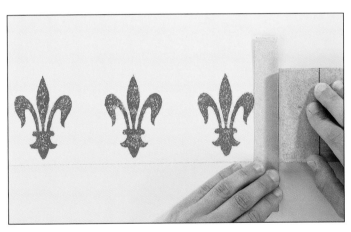

4 A piece of card (stock) held between the previous print and the stamp will ensure that there is consistent spacing between the motifs.

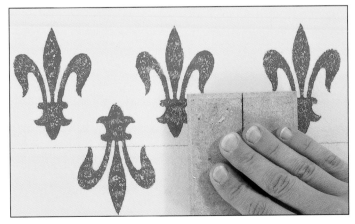

5 For a tighter design, butt the stamped motifs together without any spacing.

6 Once the paint is dry, the pencil guideline can be removed using a clean cloth wrung out in soapy water and rubbed along the line.

STAMP EFFECTS

Although basic stamping is a very simple and straightforward technique, you can achieve many different and subtle effects with stamps, depending on the paint mixture you use and the way in which it is applied. The same stamp, cut from high-density sponge, was used to make all the following prints.

Half-shade

Roll the first, paler colour over the stamp, then roll a second, darker shade over one half only, to create a three-dimensional shadowed effect.

Two-tone

Using a paintbrush, load the stamp with the first colour, then apply the second colour to the top and bottom edges only.

Two-tone with dry roller

For an even subtler colour mix, roll the second colour right over the first using a very dry roller.

Contrasting detail

To pick out details of the design in a contrasting colour, apply the first colour with a roller, then use a paintbrush to apply the second contrasting colour in the areas you want.

Partial outline

This shadow effect is produced by stamping the motif in one colour, then partially outlining the print using a paintbrush or felt-tip pen. For a natural shadow effect, place all the shadow on either the right-hand or left-hand side.

Drop shadow

Another, very subtle, effect of shadows and highlights can be produced by stamping the motif in the darker colour first. When this is dry, load the stamp with the paler colour and print over the first image, positioning the stamp slightly to one side.

Stippled

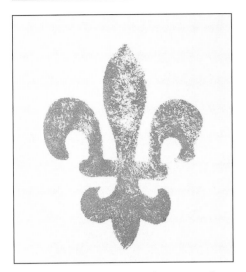

This stippled effect gives the stamped print lots of surface interest. Apply the paint with a stiff paintbrush and a dabbing, stippling motion.

Wallpaper paste

Adding wallpaper paste to emulsion (latex) paint gives the stamped print a translucent, watercolour quality.

Light shadow

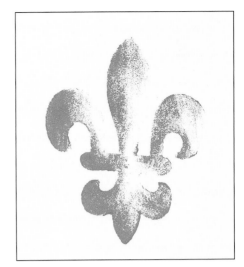

Here the paint has been applied with a roller, covering each element of the motif more heavily on one side to create a delicate shadow effect.

Second print

After loading the stamp with paint, print first on a piece of scrap paper. This very delicate image is the second print.

Sponge print

Apply a sponge print in one colour over a rollered colour in another colour for a different effect, as shown here.

Distressed

A single colour of paint applied with a dry roller produces an aged, distressed paint effect.

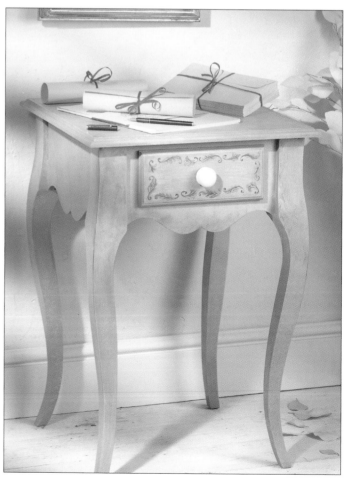

THE
PROJECTS

The following pages consists of twenty-six step-by-step inspirational projects, each focusing on a different household object. You can follow the steps for the projects exactly or use elements from them, adapting them to your own style – you will soon transform your furniture and home accessories into something decorative and unique.

DISTRESSED TABLE TOP

A second-hand buy can be transformed with a fashionably distressed look in shades of blue paint. Petroleum jelly and candle wax resist the paint in different ways. The petroleum jelly is applied to the table top in the main areas of natural wear and tear; the candle wax is then used, giving a more subtle effect.

You will need

- sanding block and medium-grade abrasive paper
- emulsion (latex) paint in navy blue, pale blue and mid-blue
- small decorator's paintbrush
- petroleum jelly and brush
- clean cotton cloth
- candle
- matt (flat) acrylic varnish and brush

1 Sand the table top to provide a key for the paint.

2 Paint with the navy blue emulsion (latex). Leave to dry.

3 Brush blobs of petroleum jelly on to the table top, working inwards from the edges of the table.

4 Paint the table top with pale blue emulsion, applying the brushstrokes in the same direction – don't cover the surface completely. Leave to dry.

5 Wipe over with a cloth and soapy water. In the areas where the petroleum jelly has been applied, the pale blue paint will come away, revealing the navy blue base coat.

6 Rub over the surface of the table with candle wax, concentrating on the edges of the table top and areas where there would be natural wear and tear.

7 Paint the table with mid-blue emulsion, again applying the brushstrokes in the same direction. Leave to dry.

8 Rub over the surface with abrasive paper. Where the candle wax has been applied, the mid-blue paint will be removed. Seal the table with two coats of varnish.

DRY-BRUSHED CHAIR

A soft, distressed look is achieved by dry brushing off-white paint over a light brown base painted to imitate wood. This is another excellent technique for making a tired old piece of furniture look desirably aged.

You will need

- clean cotton cloth
- sanding block and medium-grade abrasive paper
- emulsion (latex) paint in pale terracotta and off-white
- small decorator's paintbrush
- sponge
- matt (flat) acrylic varnish and brush

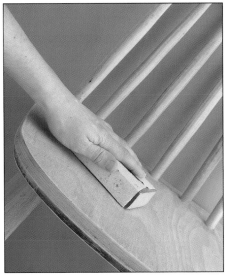

1 Wipe over the chair with a damp cloth, then sand it in the direction of the grain.

2 Mix the pale terracotta emulsion (latex) 50/50 with water. Paint the whole chair.

3 While the paint is still wet, use a sponge dampened with water to remove the excess paint mixture carefully.

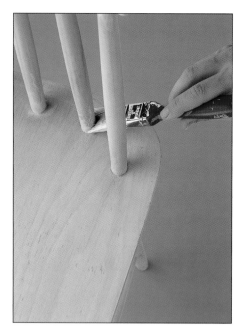

4 Using a dry brush, apply the off-white emulsion over the chair. At the angles, flick the paint from the base upwards.

5 For the flat surfaces, hold the brush at an angle and apply the paint with minimal pressure. Leave to dry then seal with two coats of varnish, leaving to dry between coats.

GRAINED DOOR

This strongly textured combed graining is achieved by mixing wall filler with sky blue emulsion (latex). Lime green paint is then brushed over the blue and sanded off when dry to give a surprisingly subtle effect.

You will need

- medium-grade abrasive paper
- emulsion (latex) paint in sky blue and lime green
- medium decorator's paintbrush
- wall filler
- rubber comb
- matt (flat) acrylic varnish and brush

1 Using medium-grade abrasive paper, sand the door to provide a key for the paint. Paint the surface with a base coat of sky blue emulsion (latex). Leave to dry.

2 Mix 25 per cent filler with 75 per cent sky blue paint. Paint on, working on a small section at a time. While still wet, comb lines, following the grain. Leave to dry.

3 Paint the door with a thin coat of lime green emulsion, applying the paint in the same direction as the combing to follow the grain of the wood. Leave to dry.

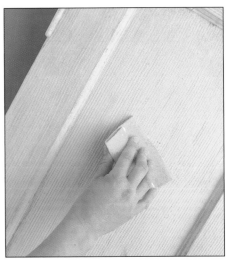

4 Sand the door, revealing lines of sky blue paint beneath the lime green top coat. Seal with two coats of acrylic varnish.

HARLEQUIN SCREEN

Two simple paint techniques – stippling and rag rolling – are used here to great effect. Choose bright shades of paint as the colours will be softened by the white-tinted scumble glaze.

You will need

- three-panel screen with curved top
- screwdriver
- emulsion (latex) paint in cream
- medium decorator's brush
- fine-grade abrasive paper
- 1cm/½in wide masking tape
- 1cm/½in wide flexible masking tape
- long ruler or straight piece of wood
- water-soluble marker pencil
- fine line tape or car striping tape
- wide easy-mask decorator's tape
- stencil brush
- kitchen paper
- white palette or old white plate
- emulsion (latex) paint in turquoise, red, yellow and green
- matt (flat) varnish and brush
- acrylic paint in white
- acrylic scumble
- clean cotton cloth
- acrylic paint in gold
- gouache paint in gold
- small stencil brush

PREPARATION

It is best to remove the hinges before sanding the surfaces to be decorated. Apply cream emulsion (latex) and leave to dry, then sand to give a smooth surface. Refer to the artwork at the back of the book for templates of how to mark up the screen.

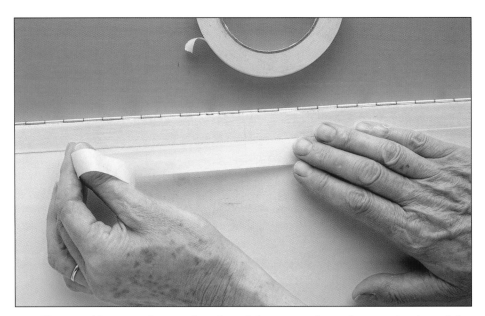

1 Place masking tape close to the edge of the screen along the outer borders of the two outer panels, and along the base of all three panels. Place a second line of tape next to the first.

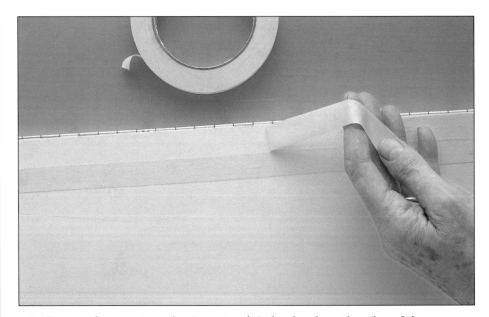

2 Remove the outer tape, leaving a 1cm/½in border along the edge of the screen. Smooth down the remaining tape. Using flexible masking tape, repeat steps 1 and 2 along the top of all three panels.

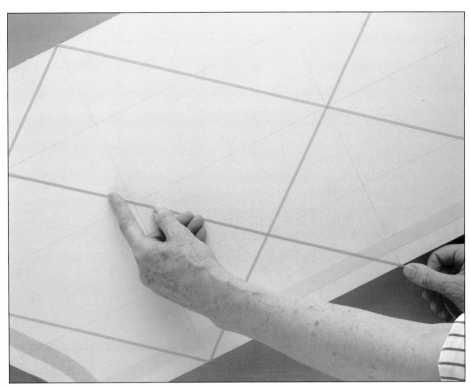

3 Measure the height of the screen at the longest point and divide by six. Draw a vertical line halfway across the panel. Mark the centre point and two equally spaced points either side. Return to the centre point and divide the panel horizontally into four equal points, one each side of the central line. Draw a grid of equal-sized oblongs, four across and six down. Repeat for the other panels.

4 Lay fine line tape or car striping tape from the centre point at the top of each panel diagonally to the far right-hand corner of the next space. Continue from the far right-hand corner through the centre point until all the lines are marked with tape. Repeat in the opposite direction to make a diamond pattern. Secure the tape at the sides of the panel with a small piece of masking tape.

5 Using wide easy-mask decorator's tape, mask off the diamonds that are to be painted in the first colour. Follow the picture of the finished screen for colour reference.

6 Bind 2.5cm/1in at the base of the stencil brush with masking tape. Dip the brush into the first colour, wipe the surplus on kitchen paper until the brush is fairly dry, then stipple the masked diamonds. Work out to the masking tape, using a firm pouncing motion. Leave to dry. Using the other colours, stipple all the diamonds in the same way.

8 Holding a crumpled cloth between both hands, roll it down each panel while the glaze is still wet, moving your hands in different directions. Leave the glaze to dry.

7 When all the paint is dry, remove the fine line or car striping tape. Apply a coat of matt (flat) varnish and leave to dry. Mix a little white acrylic paint into the scumble to make a glaze. Paint this over the diamonds.

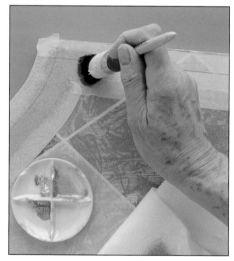

10 Mix both gold paints together. Lay masking tape either side of the cream borders. Stipple the gold paint on with a small stencil brush. Leave to dry, then remove the masking tape. Apply a final coat of varnish. When dry, replace the screen hinges.

9 Apply another coat of varnish. When this is dry, remove the masking tape from the borders of the diamonds.

SCANDINAVIAN TABLE

This pretty little table has been distressed by rubbing back thin layers of colour with fine wire (steel) wool. Focusing on the areas that would normally suffer most from general wear and tear gives an authentic aged look. The simple leaf design is painted freehand and picked out with paler highlights.

You will need

- MDF (medium-density fiberboard) or wooden table with drawer
- rubber gloves
- fine wire (steel) wool
- emulsion (latex) paint in dark yellow, grey-green, white, mid-green and pale green
- flat artist's paintbrush
- small decorator's paintbrushes
- acrylic scumble
- fine artist's paintbrush
- clear matt (flat) acrylic varnish and brush

1 Rub down the table with fine wire (steel) wool, wearing a pair of rubber gloves. Pay particular attention to the bevelled edges.

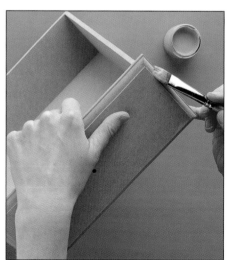

2 Using dark yellow emulsion (latex) and a flat artist's paintbrush, paint the mouldings (if any) around the edge of the drawer and the table top.

3 Paint the rest of the table and the drawer front with two coats of grey-green emulsion, allowing the paint to dry between coats.

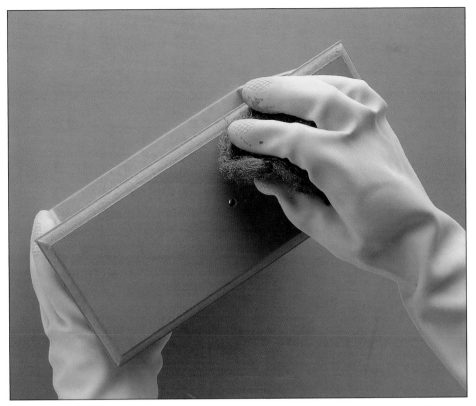

4 Wearing rubber gloves once again, rub down the entire surface of the table with wire wool. Concentrate on the areas that would naturally suffer from wear and tear.

5 Mix 50/50 white emulsion and scumble. Apply sparsely to the grey-green areas with a dry brush, using light diagonal strokes and varying the angle of the brush to give an even coverage over the surface.

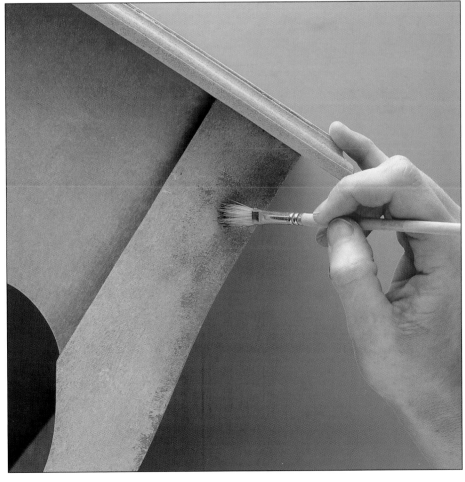

6 Mix 50/50 dark yellow emulsion and scumble. Paint this over the mouldings.

7 Apply light dabs of mid-green paint to the parts of the table that would receive the most wear: the top corners of the legs and underneath. Leave to dry, then rub back with wire wool.

8 Using a fine artist's paintbrush, paint a scrolling leaf design around the edge of the drawer front in pale green. Pick out the stalks and leaf veins with fine brushstrokes in mid-green.

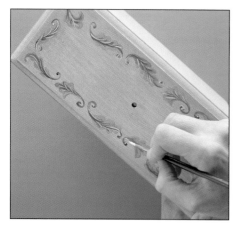

9 Still using the fine artist's paintbrush, add white and dark yellow highlights to the leaf design. Leave to dry.

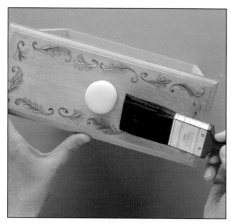

10 Seal the drawer and table with a coat of clear matt (flat) acrylic varnish for protection.

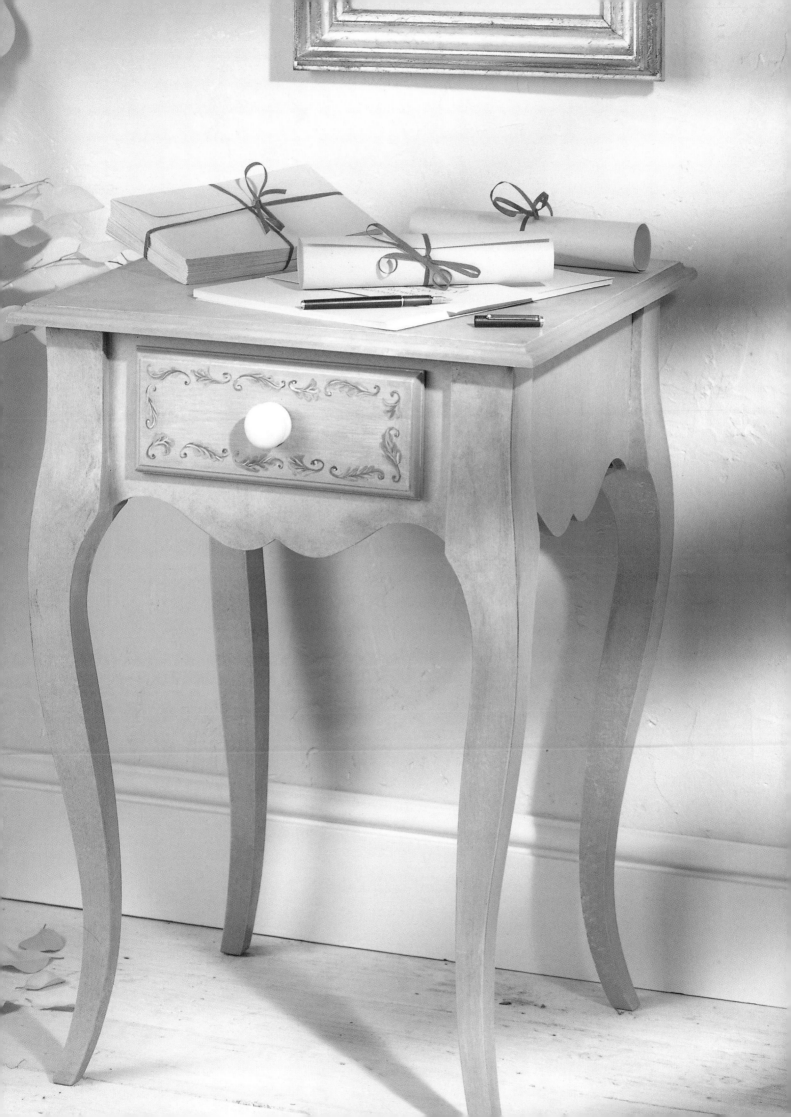

FOLK-ART CHAIR

Simple repeating designs on a white painted chair have a wonderfully naïve charm. Stick to a few bright colours in keeping with the folk-art style of this design, which any slight irregularities in the stamping will only serve to enhance.

You will need

- medium-grade abrasive paper
- wooden chair
- matt emulsion (flat latex) paint in white
- medium decorator's paintbrushes
- medium-density sponge, such as a kitchen sponge
- felt-tipped pen
- coin
- cork from a wine bottle
- craft knife
- pencil
- ruler
- acrylic paint in black, red, terracotta and blue
- paint-mixing container
- scrap paper
- clear acrylic varnish and brush

1 Sand the chair with medium-grade abrasive paper to remove any rough patches or old paint or varnish.

2 Paint the chair with two coats of white emulsion (latex) paint, allowing the paint to dry between coats.

3 Copy the heart and leaf from the back of the book. Draw around the templates on to the sponge using a felt-tipped pen. Draw around a coin on to the end of a cork to make the spot stamp.

4 Cut out the excess sponge around the motifs using a craft knife. Cut out the cork spot motif.

▶

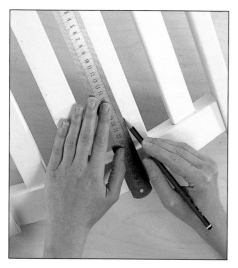

5 Using a pencil and ruler, mark the positions of the leaves, 6cm/2½in apart, on the struts of the chair back and on the seat.

6 Load the leaf stamp with black acrylic paint, then stamp once on a piece of scrap paper to remove excess paint. Stamp along the struts at a 45 degree angle. Alternate the direction of the leaves on each strut.

7 Load the heart stamp with red acrylic paint, remove the excess paint as before and stamp a heart at the top of each vertical strut, across the back and front of the chair.

8 Load the cork with terracotta acrylic paint, remove the excess paint as before and stamp a dot between each leaf shape.

9 Wash the terracotta paint off the cork, load it with blue and stamp dots 2cm/¾in apart along the legs and all round the edge of the chair.

10 Leave the paint to dry, then apply two coats of clear acrylic varnish to protect the design. Allow the varnish to dry between coats.

STARRY CABINET

Turn a junk-shop find into a unique bedside cabinet using a palette of fresh colours and a simple star motif. Before you start to paint, divide the piece visually into blocks, each of which will be a different colour, with another shade for the frame. Keep all the colours in similar tones to achieve this pretty, sugared-almond effect.

You will need

- medium-grade abrasive paper
- wooden cabinet
- wood filler
- acrylic wood primer
- medium and small decorator's paintbrushes
- emulsion (latex) paint in green, pink, blue and yellow
- wooden knobs
- star rubber stamp
- stamp inkpads in a variety of colours
- drill and drill bit
- screwdriver and screws
- masking tape
- acrylic spray varnish

1 Sand the cabinet to remove any rough patches or old paint or varnish. Fill any holes with wood filler and sand down again. Paint the cabinet with a coat of acrylic wood primer and leave to dry.

2 Paint the cabinet using several different coloured emulsion (latex) paints and allow to dry.

3 Using an assortment of all the colours except that of the frame, paint a row of spots around the edge.

4 Paint the wooden knobs. When the paint has dried, stamp a contrasting star motif on each one using coloured inkpads. When dry, drill screw holes and screw the knobs into position.

5 Stamp a contrasting star motif on to each of the spots around the cabinet frame.

6 Use masking tape to mark out a row of stripes along the bottom of the cabinet and paint them in a contrasting colour, using a fine paintbrush.

7 When all the paint is dry, protect it with a coat of acrylic spray varnish. Leave to dry thoroughly.

GRAINED WINDOW FRAME

Here, extra interest is added to a window frame by decorating it with a subtle imitation wood pattern. The same treatment would work well on a wide picture frame. To hide a boring view, stencil the panes of glass with frosted stars.

You will need

- medium-grade abrasive paper
- vinyl silk paint in pale blue-green
- medium decorator's paintbrush
- matt emulsion (flat latex) paint in deep blue-green
- water-based scumble
- heart grainer (rocker)
- clean cotton cloth
- gloss acrylic varnish and brush
- rubber comb
- star stencil
- masking tape
- stencil brush
- acrylic frosting varnish

1 Sand the window frame with medium-grade abrasive paper, then paint with pale blue-green vinyl silk paint and leave to dry. For the glaze, mix 1 part deep blue-green emulsion (latex) to 6 parts scumble. Paint the glaze over the main surfaces.

2 While the glaze is wet, draw the heart grainer (rocker) across the glazed surface, rocking it backwards and forwards. Wipe the corners with a damp cloth to make a mitre. As you work, protect the wet graining with a piece of abrasive paper. Leave to dry.

3 Apply a coat of varnish only over the glazed areas and leave to dry. Paint the inner edges of the frame and the glazing bars across the window with glaze. While still wet, draw down each piece of wood with a rubber comb. Leave to dry, then apply another coat of varnish over the whole window frame.

4 Make sure that the glass is clean, then attach the stencil with masking tape. Using a stencil brush, apply the frosting varnish evenly through the stencil. Remove the stencil before the varnish dries completely.

WAX-RESIST SHUTTERS

Give new wooden shutters or doors a weatherworn look by applying wax between two layers of different-coloured paint. Two colourways are shown – creamy yellow beneath bright blue, and pastel blue over candy pink for a sunny Caribbean feel.

You will need

- acrylic primer in white
- medium and small decorator's paintbrushes
- matt emulsion (flat latex) paint in soft yellow and bright blue or candy pink and pale blue
- neutral wax
- medium-grade abrasive paper

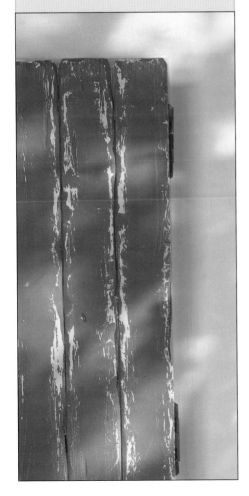

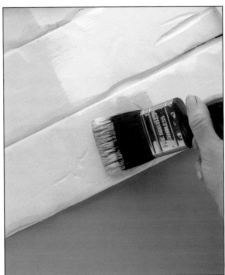

1 Paint the shutters with a coat of white primer and leave to dry. Then paint with soft yellow emulsion (latex). Leave to dry.

2 Using a small decorator's paintbrush, apply wax in areas that would naturally receive wear and tear such as the edges of the boards. Leave to dry.

3 Paint all over the shutters with bright blue emulsion, covering the waxed areas. Leave to dry.

Sand over the waxed areas to reveal the yellow base colour and create the "worn" effect.

ALTERNATIVE COLOURWAY

ABOVE: For an alternative colourway, apply candy pink matt emulsion (flat latex) paint over the primer.

ABOVE: Apply wax as described in step 2, then paint with a pale blue top coat. Rub back with abrasive paper to reveal pink areas.

VINEGAR-GLAZED FLOORCLOTH

Painted floorcloths were fashionable with the early American settlers, and they remain popular as inexpensive, handmade alternatives to carpets. This one is painted with vinegar glaze and decorated with patterns, using a cork and other simple objects as stamps. Dark shellac gives the finished floorcloth an antique finish.

You will need

- heavyweight cotton duck canvas (from artist's suppliers), 7.5cm/3in larger all round than the finished floorcloth
- staple gun or hammer and tacks
- acrylic wood primer in white
- large and medium decorator's paintbrushes
- fine-grade abrasive paper
- set square (T square)
- pencil
- large scissors
- PVA (white) glue and brush
- 2.5cm/1in masking tape
- dessertspoon
- emulsion (latex) paint in bright red
- gloss acrylic floor varnish and brush – use matt (flat) acrylic varnish if preferred
- 1cm/¹/₂in masking tape
- malt vinegar
- sugar
- bowl and spoon
- powder pigment in dark ultramarine
- reusable putty adhesive
- clean cotton cloth
- craft knife
- cork
- dark shellac and brush
- floor varnish and brush

PREPARATION

Before beginning this project, stretch the canvas across an old door or table top and staple or tack it in place. Paint the surface with three or four coats of primer, leaving to dry between coats, then sand to give a completely smooth surface. Using a set square (T square), check that the canvas is square – if not, trim it down. Mark a pencil border 2.5cm/1in from the edge. Cut diagonally across each corner, through the point where the pencil lines cross.

1 Fold over each edge to the pencil line. Glue and then secure with masking tape until dry. Rub the edges firmly with a dessertspoon. Sand the edges where the primer has cracked.

2 Turn the canvas to the right side. Using masking tape, mark a wide border. Paint with bright red emulsion (latex), carrying the paint over the outer edges. When dry, apply a coat of floor varnish. Leave to dry.

3 Remove the masking tape and tidy any ragged edges with extra paint. When dry, place 1cm/¹/₂in masking tape around the outer edge to a depth of 1cm/¹/₂in. Repeat around the inner edge of the border.

4 Mix 150 ml/¼ pint/⅝ cup malt vinegar with 1 teaspoon sugar. Add up to 2 tablespoons of dark ultramarine powder pigment and stir well – the glaze should be of a consistency to flow on smoothly. Paint the glaze over the top of the red border.

5 While the dark ultramarine glaze is still wet, make patterns by pressing the reusable putty adhesive on top and then removing it.

6 Copy the patterns shown in the illustrations or experiment with your own. Wipe the glaze with a damp cotton cloth if you make a mistake. The glaze will take about 15 minutes to dry.

7 Using a craft knife, cut a hole in one end of the cork. Paint the dark ultramarine vinegar glaze over the centre panel. While the glaze is still wet, stamp a pattern of circles and lines.

8 Cut a square at the other end of the cork to make a different stamp. Experiment with other objects. Use the reusable putty adhesive to make additional lines and curves.

9 When the glaze is dry, remove the masking tape. Tidy the edges with a damp cloth wound around your finger. Apply a coat of dark shellac, then several coats of floor varnish, allowing the canvas to dry between coats. Leave the floorcloth for at least 4 days before walking on it.

CRACKLE-GLAZE PICTURE FRAME

This simple picture frame – which could also be used to hold a small mirror – is made from a piece of plywood. Simply cut a square from the centre and edge with beading. As well as being treated with crackle glaze, the brightly coloured paintwork is distressed slightly with abrasive paper to give a very attractive finish.

You will need

- emulsion (latex) paint in yellow ochre, turquoise, orange, lime green and bright pink
- medium and small decorator's brushes
- acrylic crackle glaze
- masking tape
- craft knife
- flat artist's paintbrush
- coarse-grade abrasive paper
- acrylic varnish and brush

1 Paint the frame with two coats of yellow ochre emulsion (latex), allowing each to dry. Brush on a coat of crackle glaze. Leave to dry according to the manufacturer's instructions.

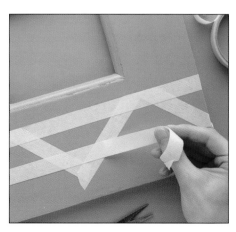

2 Place strips of masking tape in a pattern on either side of the frame, as shown.

3 Where the ends of the masking tape overlap, carefully trim off the excess tape with a craft knife.

4 Brush turquoise paint on the unmasked sections of the frame, working in one direction. The crackle effect will appear almost immediately. Take care not to overbrush an area (see Painting Techniques).

5 Brush orange paint on alternate sections of the pattern in the same way. Paint the remaining sections lime green. Leave to dry.

6 Carefully peel away the masking tape, revealing the yellow ochre base coat.

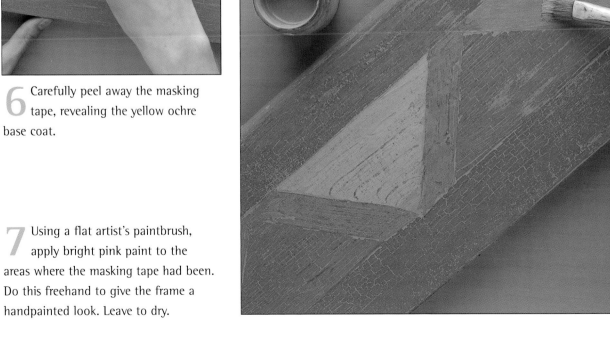

7 Using a flat artist's paintbrush, apply bright pink paint to the areas where the masking tape had been. Do this freehand to give the frame a handpainted look. Leave to dry.

8 Rub coarse-grade abrasive paper
over the whole of the picture frame
to show some of the yellow ochre paint
beneath the brightly coloured surface.

9 Seal the frame with two coats of
acrylic varnish. Apply the first coat
quickly, taking care not to overbrush and
reactivate the crackle glaze.

SPONGED LAMP BASE

Three shades of green paint are sponged on to this inexpensive lamp base to give a very attractive dappled surface. If you prefer, you can practise the sponging technique first on a piece of white paper until you are confident. You will quickly discover that it is not at all difficult, despite the very professional-looking result.

1 Cover the electric cord and bulb fitting with layers of masking tape to protect them while you work.

2 Wearing rubber gloves, rub down the existing varnish or paint with wire (steel) wool.

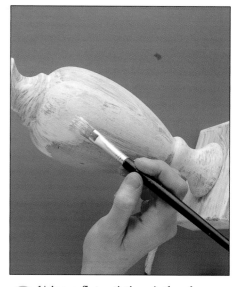

3 Using a flat artist's paintbrush, paint the lamp base with two coats of acrylic primer, leaving each to dry.

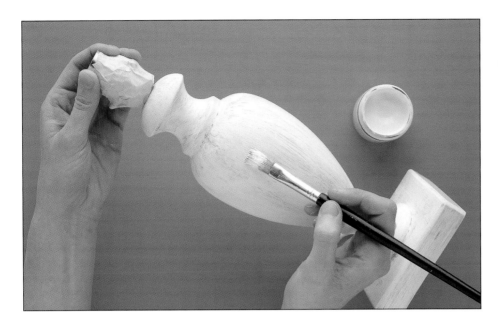

4 Paint with two coats of off-white emulsion (latex), leaving the paint to dry between coats.

5 Mix a 50/50 solution of jade green emulsion paint and water. Dampen the sponge and squeeze it until nearly dry, then dip it into the paint. Practise by dabbing the sponge on to a piece of white paper.

6 Cover the lamp base with a dappled layer of paint, applying it just a little at a time in order to build up the texture gradually.

7 Add some off-white paint to
lighten the jade green colour.
Sponge this lightly over the first layer of
colour. Break off a small piece of sponge
and use this to work the colour into the
moulding to ensure that the whole lamp
base is evenly covered.

8 Mix a little emerald green paint
50/50 with water. Apply this
mixture sparingly over the surface of
the lamp base to add extra depth and
texture. When dry, seal with three coats
of varnish, allowing the varnish to dry
thoroughly between coats. Finally,
remove the protective masking tape
from the electric cord and bulb fitting.

CRACKLE-GLAZE PLANTER

Here, crackle glaze is sandwiched between dark and pale layers of emulsion (latex) paint to give a modern planter an authentic antique look. The handpainted line is easier to do than you might think, and gives a smart finishing touch.

You will need

- MDF (medium-density fiberboard) planter
- fine-grade abrasive paper (optional)
- emulsion (latex) paint in mid-blue and dark cream
- small decorator's paintbrush
- acrylic crackle glaze
- fine artist's paintbrush
- clear acrylic varnish and brush

1 You do not need to prime MDF (medium-density fiberboard), but it may need sanding. Paint the inside and outside with mid-blue emulsion (latex).

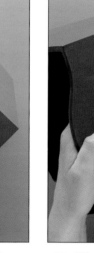

2 When the paint is completely dry, apply a layer of crackle glaze to the outside of the planter. Leave to dry.

3 Paint the outside of the planter with dark cream emulsion. The crackled effect will start to appear almost immediately, so work quickly, with regular brushstrokes. Leave to dry.

4 Holding your finger against the edge for support, paint a thin mid-blue line 1.5cm/⅝in from the edge on each side of the planter. Leave to dry, then seal with two coats of varnish.

FROSTED VASES

Give coloured or clear glass vases the designer touch using glass etching cream and reverse stencilling. The shapes are cut from sticky-back plastic and removed after stencilling to reveal the clear outlines. Choose flowers and leaves, stripes or spots – the choice is yours. The same technique could be used to transform windows.

You will need

- glass vases
- sticky-back plastic
- scissors
- rubber gloves
- glass etching cream
- soft paintbrush

1 Wash the vase with hot soapy water to remove any grease. Leave the vase to dry. Trace the flower and leaf templates at the back of the book and transfer them on to the back of a piece of sticky-back plastic. Cut out the shapes with scissors.

2 Decide where you want to position the shapes on the vase. Remove the backing paper and stick the flower and leaf shapes in place, smoothing them down.

3 Wearing rubber gloves, paint the etching cream evenly over the outside of the vase with a soft paintbrush. Leave to dry in a warm, dust-free area for about 30 minutes.

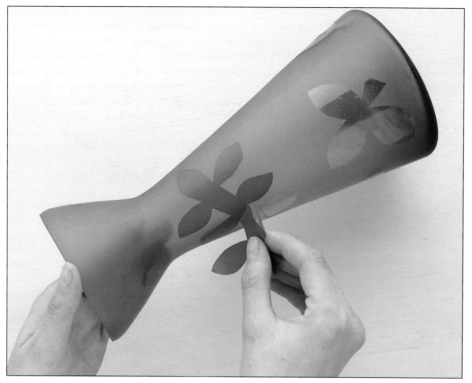

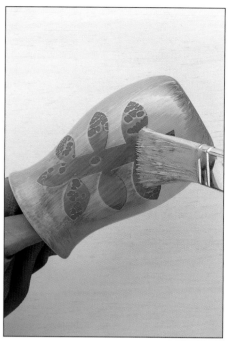

4 Still wearing the rubber gloves, wash the etching cream off the vase with warm water. Leave to dry. If there are blotchy areas where the etching cream hasn't worked, simply paint the vase again and leave for another 30 minutes before washing it off. When you are happy with the results, peel off the sticky shapes. Wash the vase again to remove any sticky smears left by the plastic.

5 For a smaller vase, try using just one motif. Paint on the etching cream in the same way as for the large vase and leave it for 30 minutes.

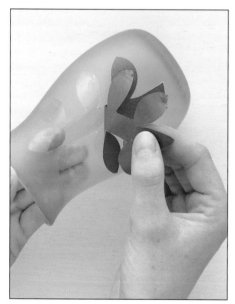

6 Wash off the etching cream and peel off the plastic motif to reveal the design, then wash the vase again. If there are any blotchy areas, paint the vase again with etching cream as in step 4.

7 For a striped frosted vase, cut out straight or wiggly strips of sticky-back plastic and stick them on to the vase. Paint on the etching cream as before and leave to dry for 30 minutes.

8 Wash off the etching cream, then peel off the plastic strips and wash the vase again to remove any sticky smears left by the plastic.

ART NOUVEAU HATBOX

An elegantly stencilled hatbox and matching shoe bag would be perfect for storing a bride's hat and shoes. Make a set for yourself or to give to someone special. And you needn't stop there: stencil a whole stack of matching hatboxes to use for stylish storage in a bedroom.

You will need

- round hatbox
- undercoat in white
- small decorator's paintbrush
- water-based woodwash in pale green
- masking tape
- tape measure
- pencil
- stencil card (stock)
- craft knife and self-healing cutting mat
- ruler
- spray adhesive
- stencil brushes
- stencil paint in dark green, royal blue and pale green

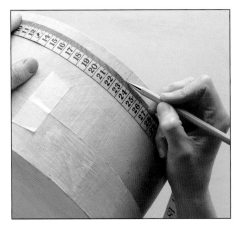

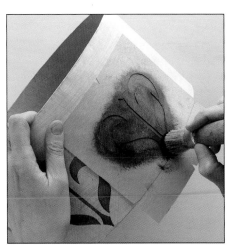

1 Paint the hatbox with two coats of white undercoat. Dilute 1 part pale green woodwash with 1 part water and apply two or three light washes to the hatbox, allowing them to dry between coats. Attach the lid with strips of masking tape. Measure the circumference of the box and divide by six or eight. Lightly mark the measurements on the lid and side of the box with a pencil.

2 Trace the templates at the back of the book. Cut the stencils from stencil card (stock) as described in Stencilling Techniques. Rule a pencil line across the bottom of the stencil to help align it on the box. Spray lightly with adhesive and position on the box. Using a stencil brush and dark green stencil paint, stencil the leaves and stem. Remove the stencil when dry, respray with adhesive and reposition. Continue to work around the box.

3 Reposition the stencil on the leaves. Add a shadow to the points where the leaves join the stem, using royal blue paint. Use a clean stencil brush to keep the colours clean. Repeat all around the box.

ABOVE: Stencil a matching calico shoe bag, using fabric paints, to protect a treasured pair of shoes.

4 Using the heart stencil, add a pale green heart between each pair of leaves around the bottom of the box.

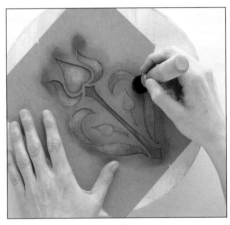

5 Stencil flowerheads around the rim of the lid in dark green following the pencil marks. Add a royal blue shadow as before. Stencil a whole flower motif in dark green in the centre of the lid.

6 Add decorative pale green heart motifs around the main motif, using a very small amount of paint for a delicate touch.

STAR FRAME

Give plain or old picture frames a new look with textured stars. Adding ready-mixed filler to acrylic stencil paint gives a three-dimensional effect to stencilled designs. Once you have mixed it you will need to work quickly before it sets.

1 Paint the frame in dark blue emulsion (latex) paint using a small decorator's paintbrush. When dry, apply a second coat and leave to dry.

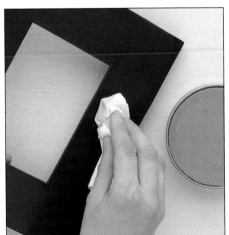

2 Using a soft cloth, rub wax furniture polish all over the frame and leave to dry. The wax will partly resist the next layer of paint.

3 Paint the frame with light blue emulsion paint and leave to dry. Paint on a second coat and leave to dry. Then lightly sand the frame to create a distressed effect.

5 Position the large star stencil on the corners of the frame and dab on the filler with a stencil brush. Add the small stars as illustrated. Leave the filler to dry and wash the brush thoroughly.

4 Trace the templates at the back of the book. Using a craft knife and self-healing cutting mat, cut a large and a small star stencil from acetate as described in Stencilling Techniques. In a bowl, mix together the ready-mixed filler and dark blue acrylic paint until you are happy with the shade, remembering that when the filler dries the colour will be much lighter.

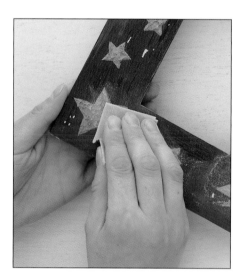

6 When the filler has dried and hardened, gently smooth over all the stars with fine-grade abrasive paper.

7 For a coordinated look, paint and stencil round or square flower pots in the same way as the picture frame.

SEASHORE BATHROOM SET

Seaside themes are always popular for a bathroom and these stencils in fresh blue and white link the different elements of the room. For best results, choose paints to suit the surface you are planning to stencil: enamel paint for plastic and glass, and fabric paint for the towels.

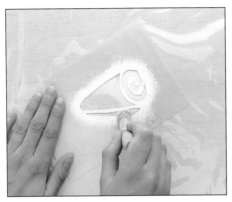

1 Trace the shell, starfish and fish templates at the back of the book. Cut the stencils from acetate as described in Stencilling Techniques. Lay the shower curtain on a flat surface. Lightly dab the stencil brush in the white enamel paint and begin to stencil the shapes on the curtain.

2 Continue to stencil the shell, starfish and fish shapes randomly over the whole shower curtain, taking care not to overload the brush with paint. Leave to dry.

3 Reposition the stencils on the painted shapes and dab on the blue paint. Leave some of the shapes white. Leave the shower curtain to dry before hanging it up in place.

4 Lay the hand towel on a flat surface. Using the fish stencil and dark blue fabric paint, stencil fish along the towel border. Position the fish one behind the other, varying the angle slightly.

5 Stencil the opposite end of the towel, arranging the fish in pairs facing each other. Iron the towel to fix the fabric paint, following the manufacturer's instructions.

6 To decorate the first glass tumbler, hold or tape the fish stencil in place and gently dab on white enamel paint. Leave to dry, then reposition the stencil and continue to stencil fish all over the glass tumbler, placing the fish at different angles.

7 Decorate the second tumbler with blue fish in the same way. The tumblers should only be used for decoration; do not apply enamel paints to surfaces that will be drunk or eaten from.

ABOVE: *Blue and white stencils work well in a plain white bathroom. You can also choose colours to coordinate with your existing decor.*

TRAY OF AUTUMN LEAVES

The rich colours of autumn leaves are captured here on a simple wooden tray. Keep to warm natural paint colours to suit the country style and simple lines of the tray. Use the templates provided or draw around your own pressed leaves.

You will need

- wooden tray
- fine-grade abrasive paper
- water-based primer (if bare wood)
- emulsion (latex) paint in blue-grey and ochre
- small decorator's paintbrush
- household candle
- clean cotton clothes
- craft knife and self-healing cutting mat
- stencil card (stock)
- spray adhesive
- stencil brush
- stencil paint in rust and terracotta
- saucer
- matt (flat) acrylic varnish and brush

1 Sand down the tray with fine-grade abrasive paper to ensure a smooth surface. If the wood is bare, paint with a water-based primer. Apply two coats of blue-grey emulsion (latex), leaving it to dry between coats.

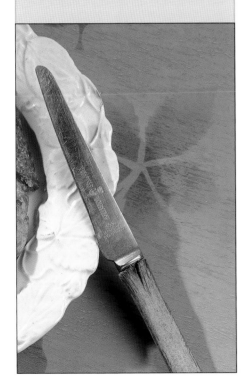

2 Rub the candle over the edges of the tray and over the base until there is a build-up of wax. Think about which areas of the tray would become worn naturally and apply wax there.

3 Wipe away any loose bits of wax with a clean cloth. Paint the whole tray with ochre emulsion. Leave to dry completely.

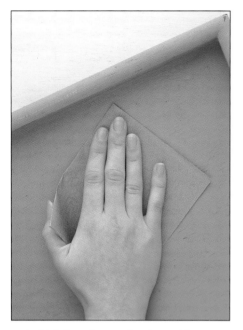

4 Lightly rub over the tray with abrasive paper to reveal some of the blue-grey paint underneath.

5 Trace the templates at the back of the book or draw around pressed leaves. Using a craft knife and self-healing cutting mat, cut out the stencils from stencil card (stock) as described in Stencilling Techniques.

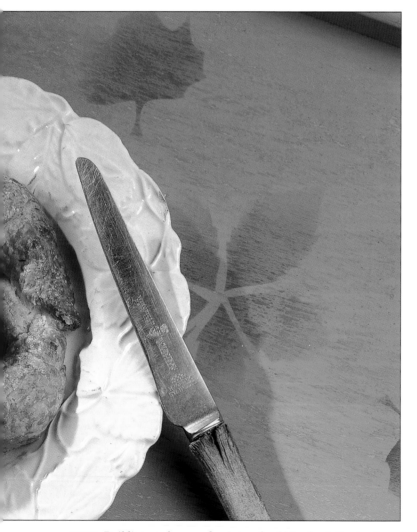

6 Lightly spray the back of the stencils with adhesive. Arrange the stencils on the tray and smooth down. Dip the stencil brush into the rust stencil paint and rub it on a saucer or cloth so that the brush is dry. Using circular movements, apply the colour evenly over the stencils, working more on one side of each motif. Apply terracotta stencil paint to the other side of the leaves to give shadow. Continue stencilling all over the tray. To give the tray a tough finish, apply two or three coats of varnish, leaving each to dry before applying the next.

ABOVE: Building up layers of paint and rubbing back the top layer in places gives the tray a pleasing distressed look.

GILDED CANDLES

Plain church candles look extra special when adorned with simple gold stars and stripes. Always associated with Christmas, candles are popular all year round for their soft romantic lighting. Cutting the stencils may be fiddly but it is then a quick job to spray on the gold paint.

You will need

- acetate
- selection of candles
- felt-tipped pen
- craft knife and self-healing cutting mat
- spray adhesive
- masking tape
- metallic spray paint

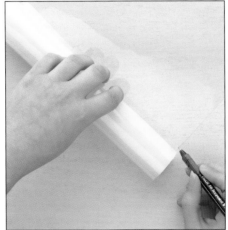

1 Wrap a piece of acetate around the candle. Mark with a felt-tipped pen and cut it to fit exactly. Do not overlap the edges. Cut it a few millimetres shorter than the candle.

2 Trace the star templates at the back of the book. Lay the piece of acetate over the stars, choosing a pattern of stars to suit the candle. Trace over them with the felt-tipped pen.

3 Cut out the stars using a craft knife and self-healing cutting mat. Be careful not to tear the acetate.

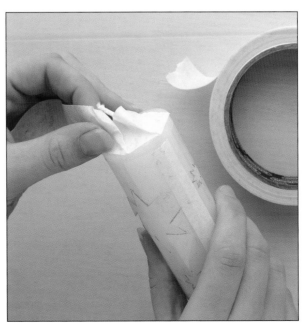

4 Spray one side of the stencil with adhesive and wrap it around the candle, centring it so that there is a small gap at either end. Secure the acetate join with masking tape. Mask the top of the candle with tape, ensuring there are no gaps.

 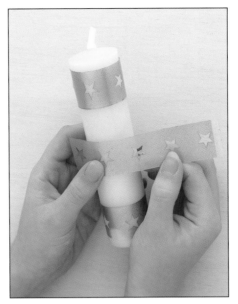 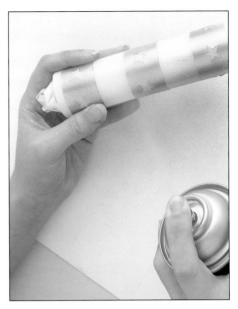

5 Spray a fine mist of metallic spray paint over the candle, holding the can about 30cm/12in from the surface. If too much paint is applied, it will drip underneath the stencil. Keep checking that the stencil is well stuck down to avoid any fuzzy lines around the stars. Leave the paint to dry for a couple of minutes, then carefully remove the masking tape and acetate.

6 For a stars and stripes candle, cut strips of acetate and trace a row of small stars along each strip. Cut out with a craft knife as before. Spray one side of the acetate strips with adhesive. Stick the strips on to the candle, measuring the gaps in between to ensure equal spacing. Secure them with small pieces of masking tape at the join.

7 Mask off the top of the candle with masking tape, ensuring there are no gaps. Spray the candle with a fine mist of metallic spray paint as in step 5. Carefully remove the masking tape and stencil when dry.

ABOVE: A basketful of gilded candles makes a pretty gift. Use a different star design on each candle.

8 For a reverse stencil design, cut out individual star shapes from acetate. Apply spray adhesive to one side, stick on to the candle and mask off the top of the candle as before. Spray with metallic spray paint and carefully remove the acetate stars when the paint is dry.

TROMPE L'OEIL PLATES

A shelf full of trompe l'oeil stencilled plates adds a witty touch to a kitchen wall. Follow this plate design or translate your own patterned china into stencils to give a coordinated look. You could add some individual plates to the wall as well.

1 Cut three pieces of stencil card (stock) 30cm/12in square. Mark the centre by measuring the centre of each edge and ruling a horizontal and a vertical line across each card to join the marks.

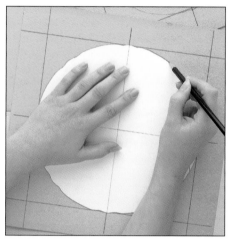

2 Draw a line 3.5cm/1¼in in from all four edges of each card. Place the plate in the centre and draw around the edge. Cut out the plate shape from the first piece of stencil card. This will be stencil 1.

3 Using a pair of compasses, draw a circle about 4cm/1½in from the edge of the plate on the two remaining pieces of card.

4 Trace or photocopy the plate template at the back of the book to the desired size and transfer to the second stencil card.

5 Cut out the design with a craft knife on a self-healing cutting mat. Cut out the smaller areas first and the larger ones last. This will be stencil 2. On the third piece of stencil card, cut out the inner circle. This will be stencil 3.

6 Draw a faint horizontal pencil line on the wall above a shelf. Add two marks 30cm/12in apart on the line to act as a guide for positioning the stencils. Spray the back of the plate stencil (1) with adhesive and place in position on the wall. Press down firmly to ensure a good contact. Mask off the surrounding area with paper and masking tape, leaving no gaps. Spray white and cream spray paint on to the stencil. Remove the masks and stencil.

7 Attach the flower stencil (2) to the wall with spray adhesive, lining it up with the marks on the wall. Mask off the surrounding area. Stick small pieces of masking tape over the leaves on the stencil. Spray the flowers with pinks and mauves, applying a fine layer of paint in short sharp puffs. Try each paint colour on the mask surrounding the stencil first to test the colour and to make sure that the nozzle is clear.

8 Remove the masking tape from the leaves. Fold a small piece of card in half and use it to shield the rest of the stencil from paint. Spray the leaves using light and dark green paints. Take care to avoid spraying paint over the flowers.

9 Cut a small hole in a piece of card and use to spray the centres of the flowers green. Use light green or dark green paint, or vary the two colours.

10 Hold the card shield around the dot designs on the border, and spray each one with red paint. Spray blue paint over the wavy lines on the border. Again, do not apply too much paint. Remove the masks and carefully remove the stencil.

11 Spray the back of the last stencil (3) with adhesive and position it on the wall. Mask off the surrounding area as before. Spray an extremely fine mist of grey paint over the top left-hand side and bottom right-hand side of the plate design to create a shadow. Aim the nozzle slightly away from the stencil to ensure that hardly any paint hits the wall. Remove the masks and stencil.

12 Reposition stencil 1 on the wall and spray a very fine mist of blue paint around the edge of the plate. Repeat for the other plates, spacing them evenly along the shelf.

SPOTTED FLOWER POTS

Customized terracotta pots will give a new, fresh look to your conservatory, patio or kitchen windowsill. Light, bright colours suit this project really well, but you can make them as subtle or as bold as you please. The end of a small sponge roller gives a neat, sharp image for the spot motifs.

You will need

- terracotta flower pots
- white acrylic primer
- medium decorator's paintbrushes
- matt emulsion (flat latex) paint in a variety of colours including yellow, white, red and blue
- paint-mixing container
- old plate
- small sponge paint rollers
- satin acrylic varnish and brush

1 Make sure the flower pots are clean and dry. Prime them with a coat of white acrylic primer and leave to dry.

2 Dilute some yellow emulsion (latex) paint with water to the consistency of single (light) cream. Colourwash the first pot using a dry brush and random brushstrokes. Allow to dry.

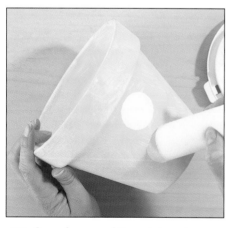

3 Spread some white paint on to an old plate. Press the end of a small sponge paint roller into the paint, then press it firmly on to the first flower pot. Remove carefully and repeat all over the pot. Leave to dry.

4 Repeat using red paint over half the white spots, but position the sponge slightly to one side of each white spot to give a highlighted three-dimensional effect. Colour the rest of the spots blue. Leave to dry.

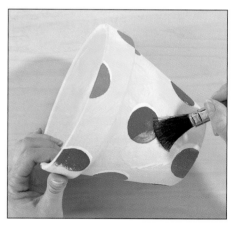

5 Repeat on the other flower pots, using different colour combinations. Seal the pots with two to three thin, even coats of satin acrylic varnish, allowing the varnish to dry between coats.

STRAWBERRY FRUIT BASKET

Strawberry motifs always look fresh and pretty, with their bright red fruits and shapely leaves, and the sponging technique used here suits the texture of strawberries particularly well. This decorative planter would look lovely on a kitchen windowsill filled with herbs or, of course, with strawberry plants.

You will need

- medium-grade abrasive paper
- wooden planter
- medium decorator's paintbrush
- matt emulsion (flat latex) paint in white
- medium-density sponge, such as a kitchen sponge
- felt-tipped pen
- scissors or craft knife and cutting mat
- pencil
- acrylic paint in red, green and yellow
- fine artist's paintbrush
- clear acrylic varnish and brush

1 Lightly sand the planter with medium-grade abrasive paper to prepare the surface for painting.

2 Apply two coats of white emulsion (latex) paint, allowing the paint to dry and sanding lightly between coats.

3 Copy the strawberry, leaf and calyx templates from the back of the book. Draw around them on the sponge with a felt-tipped pen. Cut away the sponge around the shapes using scissors or a craft knife and cutting mat.

4 Mark the positions of the strawberries on the planter in pencil. Load the strawberry stamp with red acrylic paint, then stamp the strawberries on the planter. Allow to dry.

5 Load the calyx stamp with green acrylic paint and stamp a calyx just above each strawberry shape.

6 Mark the positions of the large and small leaves on the planter. Load the leaf stamp with green paint and stamp the leaves, making the large leaves by stamping three times.

8 Use the fine artist's paintbrush to paint yellow seeds on the strawberries. When the paint is dry, apply two coats of clear acrylic varnish, all over the planter to protect the design.

7 Allow the leaves to dry, then use a pencil to mark the positions of the stems. Paint the stems freehand using a fine artist's paintbrush and green paint.

STAMPED WRAPPING PAPER

Y ou can turn plain sheets of paper into fabulous hand-printed gift wrap using simple, bold linoleum-cut motifs and coloured inks. The designs are finished off using small rubber stamps. For the chequerboard design, position the linoleum block carefully to get an even pattern. Cut up a large sheet to make gift tags, threaded with narrow ribbon.

1 Draw the star and star outline freehand on to paper. Cut out and copy on to two squares of linoleum, using a felt-tipped pen.

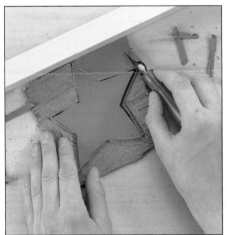

2 Butt the first linoleum square against an offcut of wood and place the wood against a wall on a flat surface, to prevent the linoleum from slipping. Cut away the area around the design using linoleum-cutting tools.

3 To cut out the spots for the star outline you will need a fine cutting tool. Place the point of the tool on a marked spot and scoop out the linoleum. Dust away the shavings.

4 Select a coloured ink for the star shape and squeeze a small amount on to a piece of glass or old saucer. Roll out the ink until it feels tacky, then roll it on to the star stamp. Do not apply too much or the linoleum will slip when printing.

5 Position the star stamp on the paper and press down, holding firmly in place. Smooth the back of the linoleum with the back of a metal spoon. Reapply the ink before printing each star.

6 Use a darker shade of ink for the star outline and line it up carefully over the plain shape. Smooth over the back of the linoleum with a metal spoon.

7 To complete the star design, use a small star-shaped rubber stamp and coloured inkpads to match the colours of the large stars. Stamp the small stars at random between the large ones. Repeat the motifs on gift tags, punch a hole with a hole punch and thread with narrow ribbon.

8 Follow the design in the picture to make a chequerboard stamp in the same way. Finish with a small spot-shaped rubber stamp on each square.

FRENCH COUNTRY KITCHEN

This curtain (drape) design is adapted from the pattern on a French Art Deco soup bowl found in a fleamarket in Brussels. The flower design is echoed in the hand-stencilled tiles and teams perfectly with the simple chequerboard border for a country look.

You will need

For the curtain (drape):

- white muslin (cheesecloth)
- iron
- newspaper
- masking tape
- stencil card (stock)
- craft knife and self-healing cutting mat
- spray adhesive
- solid stencil paint in blue
- stencil brush
- pressing cloth
- needle
- white sewing cotton
- tape measure
- dressmaker's chalk
- white cotton tape
- small pearl buttons

For the tiles:

- 10cm/4in square white tiles
- spray paint in red

MEASURING UP

To calculate the amount of muslin (cheesecloth), allow 1.5 times the width of the window plus 2.5cm/1in for each side hem, and add 7.5cm/3in to the length for hems.

1 Press the muslin (cheesecloth) to remove any creases, then fold it lengthways in accordion-style folds. Press lightly to mark creases, then fold it widthways in accordion-style folds and press again. These squares will act as a guide for positioning the motifs. Cover the work surface with newspaper and tape down the muslin so that it is taut.

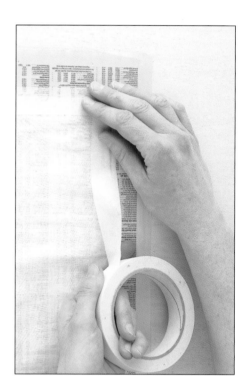

2 Trace the three floral templates and the border template at the back of the book and cut out the stencils from stencil card (stock) as described in Stencilling Techniques. Spray the back of one stencil with adhesive and, starting at the top right, lightly stencil the first motif.

3 Alternating the three floral stencils as you work, lightly stencil flowers in every other square over the whole curtain (drape), leaving 15cm/6in free at the lower edge for the border.

4 Stencil the blue chequerboard border along the bottom, lining up the stencil each time by matching the last two squares of the previous motif with the first two of the next stencil. Press the fabric well using a pressing cloth and iron.

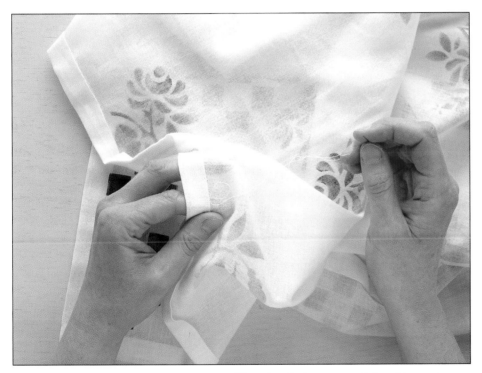

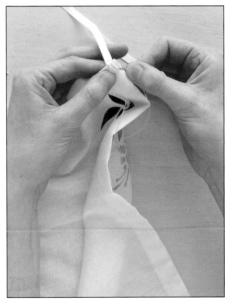

5 Press under and slip-stitch a 1.25cm/½in double hem around the sides and lower edge of the curtain. Make a 2.5cm/1in double hem along the top edge.

6 Measure the top edge of the curtain and, using dressmaker's chalk, mark it into sections about 20cm/8in apart. Cut a 25cm/10in piece of white cotton tape for each mark. Fold the first piece of tape in half and stitch to the back of the first mark. Sew a button on to the front of the curtain to anchor the tape. Repeat all the way along the edge and then tie the finished curtain on to the curtain pole in bows.

7 For the tiles, cut a piece of stencil card to fit the tile. Cut out the three floral stencils as before, using a craft knife and a self-healing cutting mat.

8 Wash the tiles in warm soapy water. Cover the work surface with newspaper. Using red spray paint, spray over the first floral stencil lightly and evenly. Leave to dry, then remove the stencil. Repeat with the other tiles, using all three stencils.

ORGANZA CUSHION

If you always thought stencilling had a simple country look, then think again. This brilliant organza cushion with gold stencilling takes the craft into the luxury class. Use the sharpest dressmaker's pins when handling organza to avoid marking the fabric.

You will need

- dressmaker's graph paper
- ruler
- pencil
- scissors
- dressmaker's pins
- organza, 1m/1⅛yd each in main colour and contrast colour
- stencil card (stock)
- craft knife and self-healing cutting mat
- spray adhesive
- masking tape
- scrap paper
- spray paint in gold
- needle and thread
- sewing machine
- iron
- 50cm/20in cushion pad

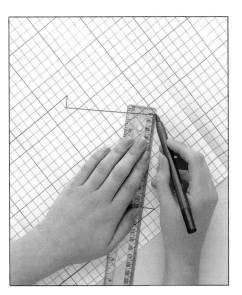

1 Copy the border template at the back of the book on to dressmaker's graph paper and cut it out with scissors. In addition, cut out a 53cm/21in square and a 53 × 40cm/21 × 16in rectangle from graph paper.

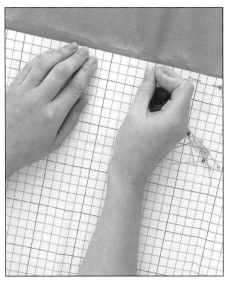

2 Pin the square and rectangle to the main colour of organza. Cut two 53cm/21in squares, and two rectangles measuring 53 × 40cm/21 × 16in. Cut four border pieces from the contrasting colour of organza.

3 Cut a piece of stencil card (stock) 18 × 53cm/7 × 21in. Trace the template and transfer to the card, 8cm/3in from the bottom edge and with 6cm/2½in to spare at each end. Cut out the stencil.

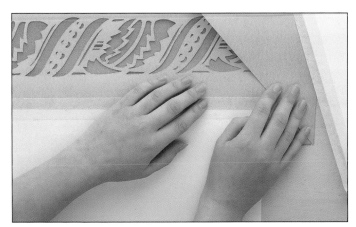

4 Spray the back of the stencil with adhesive and position it along the edge of one organza square. Cut two 45 degree mitres from stencil card, spray with adhesive and press in place. Mask off the surrounding areas with scrap paper.

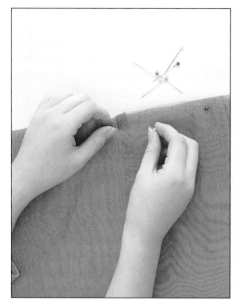

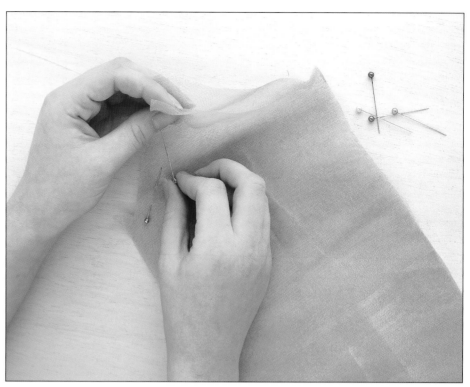

5 Spray with gold paint. Leave to dry and spray again. Remove the masking paper and stencil. Place the stencil along the next edge, put the mitres in place and continue as before. Stencil the remaining two sides. Hem one long edge of each fabric rectangle by folding over 1cm/³/₈in, then 1.5cm/⁵/₈in. Pin, tack (baste) and machine stitch the hem, then press.

6 Lay the stencilled fabric square face down and the second square on top. Lay the two rectangles on top, overlapping the stitched edges so that the raw edges line up with the squares. Pin, tack and machine stitch 1cm/³/₈in from the raw edge. Trim the seam allowance to 7mm/¹/₄in. Pin, tack and stitch the border pieces together at the mitred corners 1.3cm/¹/₂in from the raw edges. Trim the corners and turn the right way out. Press. Continue until the border pieces make a ring.

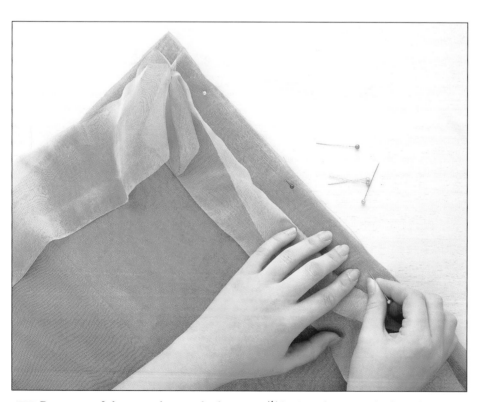

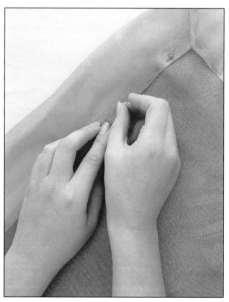

7 Press one of the raw edges under by 1.3cm/¹/₂in. Lay the pressed edge of the border fabric along the edge of the main fabric square and pin, tack and machine stitch in place.

8 Turn the cushion over and pull the border over. Turn under the border's raw edge by 1.3cm/¹/₂in and pin in place along the front of the cushion. Tack and machine stitch in place. Press. Insert the cushion pad.

TABLECLOTH AND NAPKINS

Inspiration for stencil designs can be all around you, waiting to be discovered. Cutlery and kitchen utensils are wonderful graphic shapes, ideal for stencilling. Arrange them as borders around the edge of a tablecloth and matching napkins or place the knives and forks formally on each side of imaginary place settings.

You will need

- acetate
- craft knife and self-healing cutting mat
- plain-coloured cotton napkins and tablecloth
- fabric paints in various colours
- stencil brush
- fine artist's paintbrush
- medium artist's paintbrush (optional)
- iron

1 Trace the cutlery, heart and utensils templates at the back of the book and cut the stencils from acetate. Lay one of the napkins on a flat surface. Plan your design and start to stencil the cutlery around the edge.

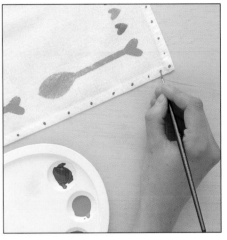

2 Stencil hearts in between the cutlery stencils. Using a fine artist's paintbrush, paint small dots around the hem of the napkins. Use different colours of fabric paint.

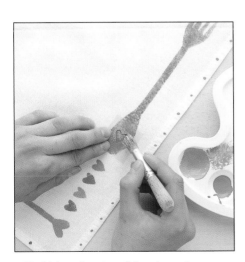

3 Using the stencil brush again, stencil hearts on the handles of some of the cutlery.

4 Stencil each napkin with a different pattern, varying the arrangement of the stencils and the colours.

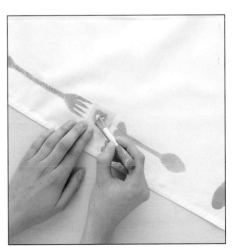

5 Lay the tablecloth on a flat surface and begin to stencil a border of cutlery and hearts.

6 Stencil the larger utensil shapes in the middle of the tablecloth. Stencil the handles first. Stencil the top of the utensils, for example the whisk, in a contrasting colour.

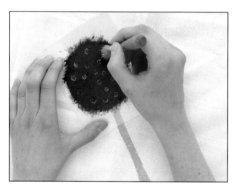

7 Stencil the draining spoons and then add the draining holes in a different colour. Use a medium artist's paintbrush if you prefer to paint the holes.

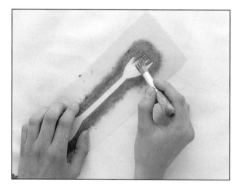

8 Fill in the blank areas around the utensils with more cutlery stencils. Leave the fabric paint to dry and then iron the reverse of the fabric to fix the paint. Fabric paints are washable so you will have no trouble laundering the tablecloth and napkins.

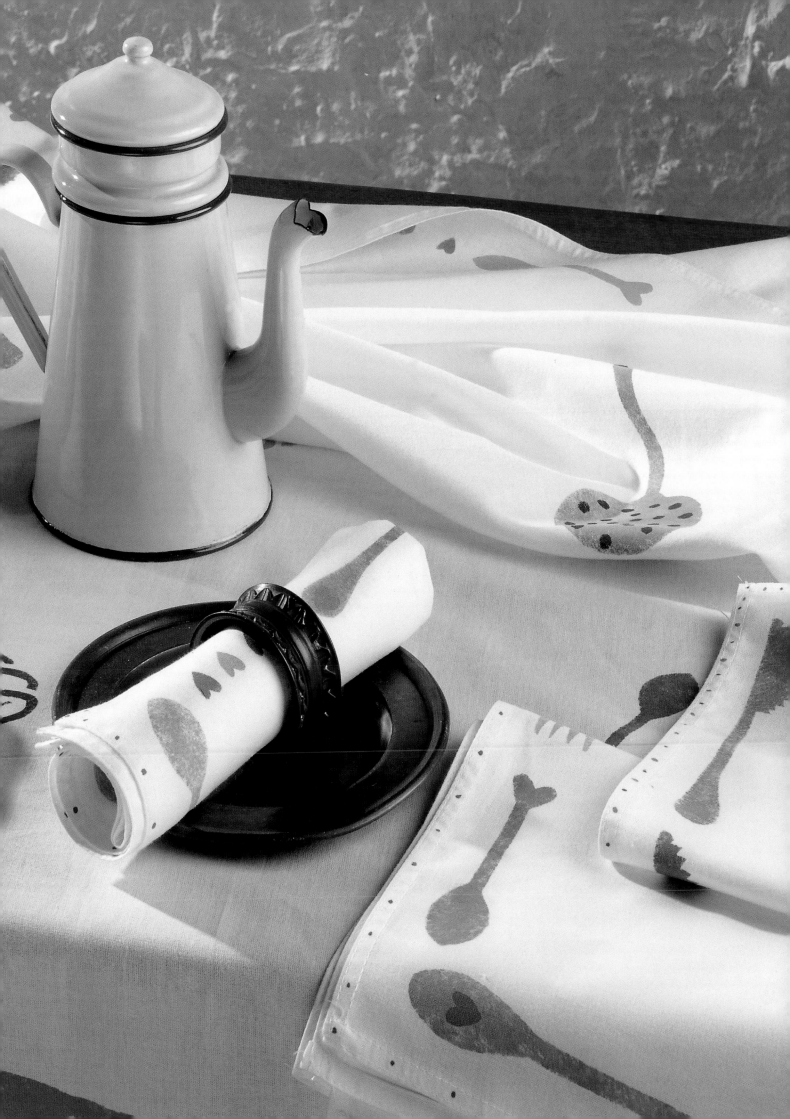

TEMPLATES

The templates on the following pages may be re-sized to any scale required. The simplest way of doing this is to enlarge or reduce them on a photocopier. Alternatively, trace the design and draw a grid of evenly spaced squares over your tracing. Draw a larger grid on another piece of paper and copy the outline square by square. Draw over the lines to make sure they are continuous.

HARLEQUIN SCREEN
(how to mark the panels and apply the masking tape)
pages 50–53

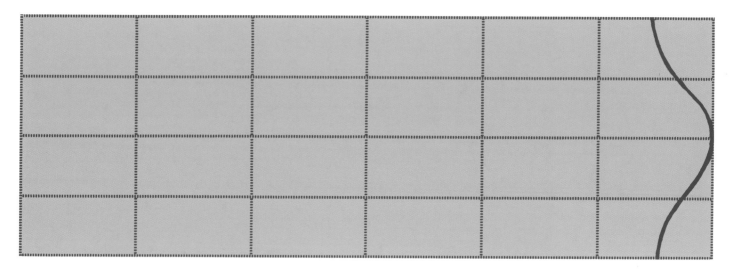

The pencil marks

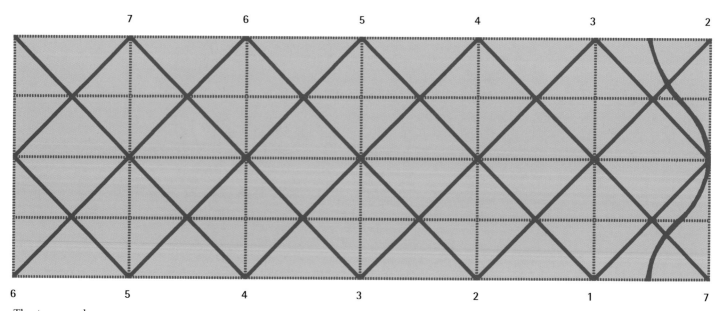

The tape marks

FOLK-ART CHAIR
pages 58–60

FROSTED VASES
pages 82–84

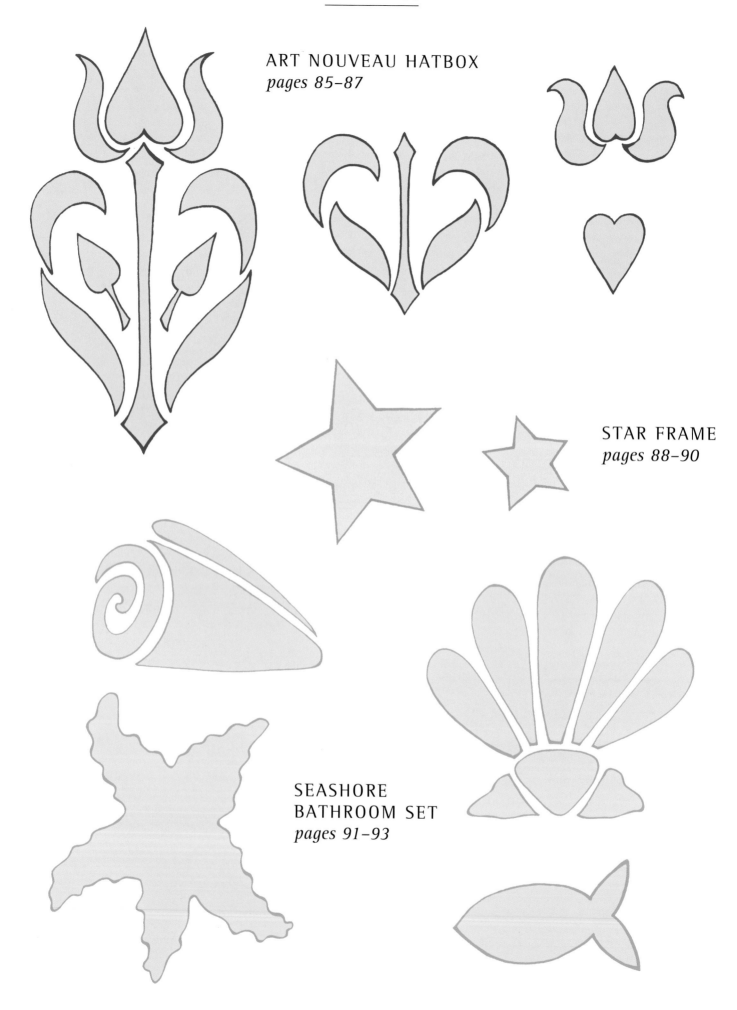

ART NOUVEAU HATBOX
pages 85–87

STAR FRAME
pages 88–90

SEASHORE
BATHROOM SET
pages 91–93

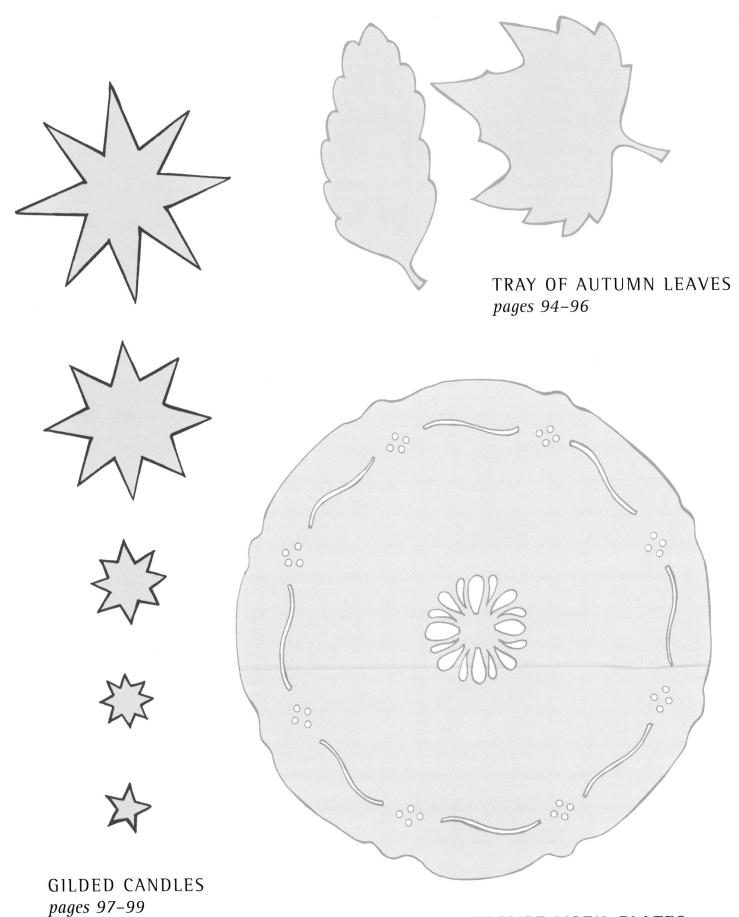

TRAY OF AUTUMN LEAVES
pages 94–96

GILDED CANDLES
pages 97–99

TROMPE L'OEIL PLATES
pages 100–103

STRAWBERRY FRUIT
BASKET
pages 106–108

FRENCH COUNTRY KITCHEN
pages 112–115

ORGANZA CUSHION
pages 116–118

TABLECLOTH AND
NAPKINS
pages 119–121

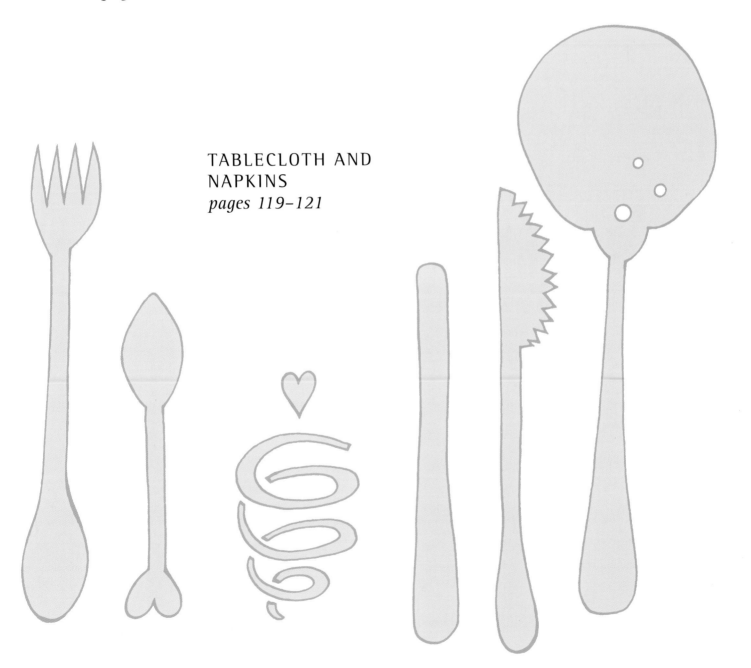

INDEX

abrasives 16
acrylics 10, 12, 14
applying paint to stamps 35
Art Nouveau hatbox 85–7, 124

basket, strawberry fruit 106–7, 126
bathrooms: seashore bathroom
    set 91–3, 124
block stencilling 29, 32
brushes 16, 18, 20, 35

cabinet, starry 61–3
candles, gilded 97–9, 125
chairs: dry-brushed chair 45–7
    folk-art chair 58–60, 123
china 36
colour 25
    mixing 26–7
colourwashing 22, 24, 25
combing 16, 22
    grained door 48–9
contrasting detail stamping 38
crackle glazing 10, 23
    crackle-glaze picture frame
        72–3
    crackle-glaze planter 80–1
craft knives 18, 20
crayons 20
curtains: French country kitchen
    112–15, 126
cushion, organza 116–18, 127
cutting mats 18
cutting stencils 28

dabbing 23, 25
designing 37
dispersion 22
distressing: crackle-glaze picture
        frame 72–3
    distressed tabletop 42–4
    Scandinavian table 54–7
    stamping 39
door, grained 48–9
dragging 23
drop shadow stamping 38
drop shadow stencilling 32
dry brush stencilling 30
dry-brushed chair 45–7
Dutch metal leaf 14

emulsion (latex) 10, 12, 14, 34
equipment 16
    painting 16–17
    stamping 20–1
    stencilling 18–19

fabric 36
fabric paints 12
flicking 30, 32
floorcloth, vinegar-glazed 69–71
flower pots, spotted 104–5
foam 14
folk-art chair 58–60, 123
French country kitchen 112–15,
    126
frosted vases 82–4, 123
frottage 22, 25

gilded candles 97–9, 125
glass 36
glazes: crackle-glaze picture
        frame 72–5
    crackle-glaze planter 80–1
    crackle-glazing 10, 23
    mixing 24, 34
    vinegar-glazed floorcloth
        69–71
gold leaf and size 12, 14
graining: grained door 48–9
    grained window frame 64–5

harlequin screen 50–3, 122
hatbox, Art Nouveau 85–7, 124
heart grainers (rockers) 16

ink pads 35
inks 14, 34
interior filler (spackle) 14, 34

kitchens: French country kitchen
    112–15, 126

lamp base, sponged 76–9
linoleum blocks 20

making stamps 33
masking tape 16, 18, 20
materials: painting 10–11
    stamping 14–15
    stencilling 12–13
measuring equipment 16, 18, 20
metallic creams 12
methylated spirits (methyl
    alcohol) 10
mixing colour 26–7
mixing paints and glazes 24, 34

napkins and tablecloth 119–21,
    127

oil-based stencil sticks and
    creams 12
organza cushion 116–18, 127

paint containers 16, 18
paint effects 10–11, 16–17,
    22–7
paints: acrylics 10, 12, 14
    emulsion (latex) 10, 12,
        14, 34
    fabric paints 12
    mixing 24, 34
    primer 10
paper: stamped wrapping paper
    109–11
partial outline stamping 38
pencils 18, 20
pens 20
picture frames: crackle-glaze
        picture frame 72–5
    star frame 88–90, 124
pigment 10
planning a design 37
planter, crackle-glaze 80–1
pre-cut stamps 14
preparing surfaces 36
primer 10

rag-rolling 23
    harlequin screen 50–3, 122
ragging 23, 24
rags 20
rollers 16, 20, 35
rotated stencilling 29, 30
rubber combs 16
rulers 20

Scandinavian table 54–7
scissors 20
screen, harlequin 50–3, 122
scumble 10
seashore bathroom set 91–3, 124
second print stamping 39
shading: stamping 38, 39
    stencilling 29, 32
shellac 10
shutters, wax-resist 66–8
sponges 16, 14, 20, 35
sponging 22, 25
    sponged lamp base 76–9
    stamping 39
    strawberry fruit basket 106–8,
        126
spotted flower pots 104–5
stamping 14–15, 20–1, 33–7
    stamped wrapping paper
        109–11
    stamp effects 38–9
star frame 88–90, 124

starry cabinet 61–3
stencil card (stock) 18
stencilling 12–13
stippling 23
    harlequin screen 50–3, 122
    stamping 39
    stencilling 31
strawberry fruit basket 107–6,
    126
surface preparation 36

tablecloth and napkins 119–21,
    127
tables: distressed tabletop 42–3
    Scandinavian table 54–7
tape measures 18, 20
templates 28
    Art Nouveau hatbox 124
    folk-art chair 123
    French country kitchen 126
    frosted vases 123
    gilded candles 125
    harlequin screen 122
    organza cushion 127
    seashore bathroom 124
    star picture frame 124
    strawberry fruit basket 126
    tablecloth and napkins 127
    tray of autumn leaves 125
    trompe l'oeil plates 125
tiles 36
    French country kitchen 112–15,
        126
tray of autumn leaves 94–6,
    125
trompe l'oeil plates 100–3, 125
two-tone stamping 38

varnishes 10, 12, 14, 34
vases, frosted 82–4, 123
vinegar-glazed floorcloth 69–71

wallpaper paste 14, 34, 39
wax 10
    wax-resist shutters 66–8
window frame, grained 64–5
wood 36
woodstain 34
wrapping paper, stamped 109–11

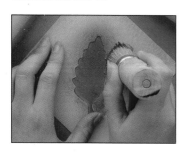